FORCING GOD'S HAND

Why Millions Pray for a Quick Rapture
----And Destruction of Planet Earth

Grace Halsell

CROSSROADS INTERNATIONAL PUBLISHING
Washington, D.C.

For additional copies of

FORCING GOD'S HAND:
Why Millions Pray for a Quick Rapture—
And Destruction of Planet Earth

Please Contact:
Crossroads International Publishing
P.O. Box 42058
Washington, D.C., 20015

Printed in the United States of America

ISBN 0-9674013-1-3

CONTENTS

PREFACE

I grew up in a small town, attending Sunday School and church services, and listening to evangelists talk about Gog and Magog, being Born Again and the fire and brimstone of Armageddon. I sensed a God of awesome power. The sermons I heard, like the West Texas sandstorms that sometimes blew to darkness, assaulted me with a mysterious force.

For many years, I accepted my Christianity as an integral part of me, as say my arms and legs, my gender, skin pigmentation. While my fundamentalism was an "integral" part of me, what was the whole? In order to better know myself, I assumed roles of "the other"—passing as a black, a Navajo Indian, a Mexican illegal.

In the 1960s, I was a staff writer at the White House when one of the Middle East wars erupted. I didn't know much about the Middle East outside the Old Testament stories. With Jimmy Carter and Ronald Reagan as Presidents, I heard more talk about Armageddon and being Born Again and, with increasing emphasis, on those who could experience the Rapture. I surfed TV channels for evangelists who, with mesmerizing zeal, preached we were a people facing the End of Time, that it was we—precisely those of us living in this very moment—who were foreordained to destroy all human history.

In my childhood, I knelt to pray at night to a God I presumed was in the sky. Yet I knew anyone who was God was too big for my small brain to define, to put into words. The stories I heard, I accepted. And stored them away in memory. In the 1980s, I wanted to know what it was I had accepted. To do so, I went on two trips to the Holy Land led by Jerry Falwell. My travels and research resulted in a book, *Prophecy and Politics*. Now, almost two decades later, I wanted to look again at what it means to be a Christian. My new inquiry led me to ask and attempt to answer pertinent questions: why does a Christian such as Jerry Falwell pray for the end of the world? Must we totally destroy this world in order to usher in a "new heaven and a new earth?"

For my inquiry into Armageddon theology, I set out with questions a "beginner" might ask.

Someone said none of us lives long enough in this lifetime to become experts or authorities, we are all novices at knowing what life—and death—is all about. Even for those of us who grow old, a life span is so short we remain amateurs. My questions and answers are for us all, the beginners.

—Grace Halsell
October, 1999

1
THE POPULARITY OF ARMAGEDDON THEOLOGY

When I was growing up, I listened to preachers relate biblical stories about enemies of God. I heard stories about Gog and Magog as allegorical, spiritual, mystical—not places I could see on a map. Today, with a Bible in one hand and a newspaper in another, Jerry Falwell and Hal Lindsey identify these enemies—and imminent invaders of Israel—as Russia and China.

Falwell and Lindsey say that God wills us to fight a terrible battle that will end human history. Now, with nearly a dozen countries possessing nuclear weapons, we can indeed exterminate the world.

The Bible, says TV evangelist Pat Robertson, "contains specific references to coming world events." It has "earthshaking prophecies." The battle of Armageddon "is now in place. It can happen any time (to) fulfill Ezekiel. It is ready to happen . . . the United States is in that Ezekiel passage, and . . . we are standing by."

"The end of the world as we know it is drawing near," writes *Final Dawn* author John Hagee. "America has become the symbol of a modern Titanic . . . we now are racing towards disaster!"

"The end is coming . . . I think it could very well happen in our lifetime," declares Pastor Ken Baugh of the McLean

Bible Church, where Special Prosecutor Kenneth Starr teaches Sunday School classes. Even before Armageddon itself, other wars will break out, Baugh warns. "One out of every two people will be killed, three billion people."

"Armageddon is a reality, a horrible reality," declares TV evangelist Jerry Falwell. "We are a part of the terminal generation, that last generation. All of history is reaching a climax . . . I don't think my children will live their full lives out." At Armageddon, Falwell says, "There will be one last skirmish and then God will dispose of this Cosmos . . . God will destroy this earth—the heavens and the earth." Billions of people, he concludes, will perish in the "holocaust of Armageddon."

Polls indicate an increasingly large number of Americans accept this theological concept. A 1984 Yankelovich poll showed that 39 percent of the American people said that when the Bible speaks of the earth being destroyed by fire, this means we ourselves will destroy our earth in a nuclear Armageddon.

By 1998, polls showed an even greater number of Americans saying the same. *Time* magazine reported that slightly more than half of the Americans—51 percent—believe that a man-made disaster will wipe out civilization during the next century.

Popular ministers who preach Armageddon theology include:

▼ Jack Van Impe of Royal Oaks, Michigan, with a weekly broadcast appearing on more than 90 UHF channels, the Trinity Broadcasting religious network, 43 U.S. radio stations and internationally on Trans-World Radio.

▼ Charles Taylor, based in Huntington Beach, California, whose "Today in Bible Prophecy" airs on more than twenty stations nationwide and globally via the Spacenet, SATCOM and Galaxy communications satellites.

▼ Stuart McBirnie, president of the unaccredited California Graduate School of Theology, who produces his own "News Commentary."

▼ Chuck Smith, whose radio program, "The World for Today," is heard on hundreds of stations and also through the Calvary Satellite Network. His 25,000-member Calvary Chapel in Costa Mesa, California spawned more than 600 other Calvary Chapels in the United States and over 100 international Calvary Chapels.

▼ Ray Brubaker, who hosts "God's News Behind the News" and offers his own magazine, *Reflections on the News.*

▼ Paul Crouch, whose Trinity Broadcasting Network (TBN) sends dooms-day prophecy shows to homes across the United States and, by satellite, around the world. Hal Lindsey is a regular guest on TBN. Crouch also has his own Saturday morning radio program in Los Angeles, and publishes the *Countdown News Journal.*

▼ James C. Dobson, a religious broadcaster in Colorado and founder of Focus on the Family, a conservative ministry with over two million members, 34 state chapters, 1,300 paid staff and an annual budget of $114 million. Via his radio

The Fastest Growing Cult in America

There's a new religious cult in America. It's not composed of so-called "crazies" so much as mainstream, middle to upper-middle class Americans. They listen—and give millions of dollars each week—to the TV evangelists who expound the fundamentals of the cult. They read Hal Lindsey and Tim LaHaye. They have one goal: to facilitate God's hand to waft them up to heaven free from all trouble, from where they will watch Armageddon and the destruction of Planet Earth. This doctrine pervades Assemblies of God, Pentecostal, and other charismatic churches, as well as Southern Baptist, independent Baptist, and countless so-called Bible churches and megachurches. At least one out of every 10 Americans is a devoteé of this cult. It is the fastest growing religious movement in Christianity today.

—Dale Crowley Jr., religious broadcaster, Washington D.C.

and television broadcasts, he reaches 28 million people a week.

▼ Luis Palau, who was featured in a front page 1999 *New York Times* article for the huge crowds he can attract. He estimates he's spoken before 12 million people in 67 nations. He has a weekly cable television program and produces three daily radio programs heard in 22 countries.

Popular ministers of Armageddon theology not only draw huge audiences, they also garner big money:

▼ Oral Roberts. The Tulsa minister once told his listeners he needed eight million dollars, "or God will call me home." His followers sent the money.

▼ W.A. Criswell. Once this pastor of the 26-thousand-member First Baptist Church of Dallas reminded his congregation that the church "has bills to pay—electricity and such." He said he needed one million dollars. He got it, in one Sunday's collection.

▼ Pat Robertson built the Christian Broadcasting Network (CBN) in Virginia Beach, which annually can collect up to $97 million in clear, tax-free profit. Within the CBN, he created the Family Channel, the nation's seventh largest cable network, featuring Robertson's popular talk show, *The 700 Club*, which, according to writer Robert Boston, "is as much about politics as it is religion." In 1997, Robertson sold the Family Channel to Fox Television for $1.9 billion.

In his biography of Robertson, *The Most Dangerous Man in America?*, Boston points out that money garnered by tax-exempt religious broadcasts financed or provided the seed money for other projects, including those of a political nature, especially the Christian Coalition. "With a $25 million annual budget, the Christian Coalition claims to have 1.7 million members and 1,600 local affiliates and chapters in all 50 states. The Christian Coalition arguably is the single most influential political organization in the U.S.," Boston reports.

Robertson, a consistent defender of the late President-Dictator Mobutu of Zaire, owns a Zaire diamond mine as well as Operation Blessing, a tax-exempt charity organization that provides flights around the world. In 1999, Virginia State

Evangelicalism

Evangelicalism, much of it still staunchly fundamentalist in doctrine, now includes approximately one-fourth of all American adults.

—William Martin, Rice University professor of sociology

Campus Crusade for Christ

Bill Bright's Campus Crusade for Christ, funded by high rollers like Nelson Bunker Hunt and T. Cullen Davis, rapidly moved toward its goal of raising a billion dollars to take the gospel to every person on the globe. Sixteen thousand Christian academies, proliferating at the rate of one a day, comprised a two-billion-dollar-a-year private education industry . . . prime-time preachers (attract) at least 20 million and garner contributions exceeding a half-billion dollars.

—Grant Wacker, *The Evangelical Tradition in America.*

Senator Janet D. Howell challenged the exemption after Operation Blessing pilots reported that some planes "were used primarily to take equipment to a diamond mine" owned by Robertson.

By 1999, Robertson, who ran for President in 1988, was moving on to becoming chairman of a big bank. His planned new national bank, affiliated with the Bank of Scotland, will have no branches, but instead deal with customers by telephone and mail. He's used the same model for accepting donations to his Christian Broadcasting Network and his political arm, the Christian Coalition. According to a March 3, 1999 *New York Times* article, Robertson will be "a very significant minority shareholder" and will be chairman of its American holding company.

"Should a foreign entity want to foster Robertson's agenda," said Andrew Killgore, former U.S. ambassador to Qatar and now president of the American Educational Trust, "Robertson's having an affiliated overseas bank will make that easy."

Books on Armageddon rival if not outsell the popularity of John Grisham novels. Hal Lindsey's *The Late, Great Planet Earth* has sold more than 25 million copies. It was a best seller all during the 1970s, outselling any other book except the Bible, and led to a movie by the same title, narrated by Orson Welles, and several sequels. Lindsey wrote four other books, including *There's a New World Coming,* all predicting that Armageddon is imminent.

In the late 1990s, evangelist Tim LaHaye's *Left Behind* series of four books dealing with the Rapture of Born Again Christians sold nearly three million copies. The popularity of the books, said a *Publishers Weekly* editor, indicates they have "crossed over from Christian to secular audiences by selling well in commercial outlets like Wal-Mart, Target and K-Mart. This says that indeed they have pervaded our culture."

▼ Bible Churches. The Dallas Theological Seminary, fountainhead of the doctrine that God demands we destroy

Planet Earth, has graduated many of the pastors now preaching Armageddon theology in nearly 1,000 Bible Churches. The Bible Churches, created in recent years all over the United States, are nondenominational—meaning they are independent of any larger body of churches. They are, however, linked within the International Fellowship of Bible Churches.

A Website reveals that states with the largest number of new Bible Churches include Michigan, New Jersey and Pennsylvania. Writing in the *Wall Street Journal* (February 12, 1999), Terry Eastland reports that many of the new Bible Churches "have spiritual links to the conservative Dallas Theological Seminary, which has produced, directly or indirectly, perhaps the majority of Bible Church pastors."

Fundamentalists number around 50 million in the United States. They are in countless Christian denominations. The most fervent advocates of Armageddon theology are in the evangelical and charismatic movements. These now represent the fastest-growing branch of fundamentalism in North American Christianity.

In these burgeoning segments of Christianity, respected theologians, pastors and seminary presidents teach the same doctrine that cult leaders such as Jim Jones told his followers as he led them to death: The End is coming soon. So let's get on with it. Let's be ahead of the crowd.

This popularity of Armageddon theology extends from the so-called "crazies" to the highest level of governmental

The Growth of Evangelical Christianity

The percentage growth of evangelical Christianity probably outstrips that of any religion in the world today, including fundamentalist Islam. We are witnessing the fastest expansion of Christianity in history, far greater than the missionary waves of the past.

—Damian Thompson, *The End of Time: Faith and Fear in the Shadow of the Millennium*

power. In his book, *With Enough Shovels: Reagan, Bush and Nuclear War,* Robert Scheer reports that Secretary of Defense Caspar Weinberger, asked in 1982 about Armageddon, replied, "I have read the Book of Revelation and yes, I believe the world is going to end—by an act of God, I hope—but every day I think that time is running out."

"The danger of Armageddon theology," says history researcher Dave MacPherson, "is that it is fatalistic and also contagious." As one example, in the late sixties and early seventies, Herbert W. Armstrong convinced thousands of his followers to surrender their assets to his Worldwide Church of God in anticipation that the world was coming to an end.

"People who expect the world to end soon do strange things," says Ted Daniels of Philadelphia, editor of *Millennium Prophecy Report* newsletter. As of 1999, Daniels had more than 1,200 cults in his database. Among such groups in the U.S. and elsewhere:

▼ Korean "Hyoo-go:" an apocalyptic group that expected 1992 to bring the removal of the righteous to heaven and the start of an apocalyptic period for the rest of the world.

▼ The "Order of the Solar Temple:" a secretive, millennial sect, that in 1994 staged a collective suicide and killing in Switzerland and Canada. Fifty persons died, some wearing medallions depicting the Four Horsemen of the Apocalypse, allegorical figures from the book of Revelation, generally interpreted to represent Christ, war, famine and death.

▼ "Branch Davidian:" cult members living outside Waco, Texas. In April 1993, Federal agents invaded their compound, with a death toll of 80 members of the apocalyptic group.

▼ "Heaven's Gate:" in 1997, thirty-nine members killed themselves in a San Diego suburb, leaving documents stating the world was evil and doomed to imminent destruction.

▼ "Voice in the Wilderness:" a millennial group in Milford, N.H., that advises against planting trees or planning ahead since the world "will not be around long enough for such activities to make sense."

▼ Elohim City: a fortress-like town near Little Rock, Ark., where some 100 heavily armed inhabitants work, pray and conduct paramilitary drills, awaiting a series of disasters they believe will end human history. Convicted Oklahoma City bomber Timothy McVeigh phoned friends in Elohim City before the 1995 Oklahoma federal building bombing.

Meanwhile, a "Christian Identity" movement, which emerged in the Reagan-Bush era, has spread in a global climate of accelerating right wing extremism. It's centered on hate of the "other"—blacks, Jews, women, gays, abortion doctors, liberals. Its theology, writes Patrick Minges in *Apocalypse Now!*, is "a unique cultural system that provides the ideological unity and theoretical framework for disparate elements of the far right, the Ku Klux Klan, neo-nazis, skinhead racists, and the 'Aryan' resistance movement."

"Identity" heroes include Randy Weaver of northern Idaho, acquitted of murdering an officer during an eleven-day standoff in August 1992, and David Koresh, whose assault by the FBI on his Texas compound was perceived by members of the far Religious Right as an "American holocaust."

In the past seven years, the Christian Identity movement has grown from around 3,000 to more than 30,000 members. Christian Identity churches have increased from a half dozen in 1986 to more than one hundred. Apart from its regular membership, it's estimated there are nearly a quarter of a million followers of the Identity movement.

ISRAEL – CENTER STAGE

2
WHAT IS ARMAGEDDON?

To learn more about Armageddon theology, I signed in 1983, along with 629 other American Christians, to go on a Jerry Falwell-sponsored tour to the Land of Christ. After landing in Tel Aviv, we board buses in groups of about 50. Then we head north, traveling to Megiddo, about 55 miles north of Tel Aviv and about 15 miles inland from the Mediterranean.

Along the way, I become acquainted with Clyde, a retired Minneapolis business executive in his late 60s. He is a college graduate and served as an Army officer during World War II. Clyde stands six feet tall, with good posture, which he credits to his service in the army.

Clyde, a widower, decided to take this trip on his own. He dresses neatly, with worsted wool trousers, white shirt, subdued tie and a cashmere jacket. He has a full head of hair, only partially gray.

At the Megiddo site, we leave the bus and walk a short distance to a tell, or mound—an artificial hill covering the successive layers of remains of ancient communities.

"An old Canaanite city once was here," Clyde remarks, adding that we are on the southern rim of the large flat expanse of the plain of Esdraelon, also called in Scripture the valley of Jezreel.

"In ancient times, Megiddo was a city of great importance. It lay at the strategic crossing of important military and caravan routes," Clyde, a history buff, says. "The Via Maris, the old coastal route linking Egypt with Damascus and the East, traversed the valley by Megiddo.

"Some historians believe that more battles have been fought here than at any other place in the world. Ancient conquerors used to say that any leader who held Megiddo could withstand all invaders.

"You read in Joshua 12:21 how Joshua and the Israelites defeated the Canaanites here in one battle," he continues. "And two centuries later the Israelite forces under Deborah and Barak—read in Judges 4 and 5—won a battle against the Canaanite captain Sisera.

"And then, as we know, King Solomon fortified the city, making it into a military center for his horses and chariots.

"Even in recent history, we've had important battles here. Near the end of the first World War, in 1918, the British General Allenby won a crucial victory over the Turks right here at Megiddo."

All the members of our party continue walking to a vantage point. We stop to absorb a commanding view of the valley of Jezreel stretching out to the northwest far into the distance.

"At last!" Clyde remarks in a voice filled with emotion, "I am viewing the site of the last great battle."

But how, I ask, did he know this was the site for Armageddon?

"You take the name—Megiddo—and add the additional Hebrew word *har,* meaning mountain, and that gives you a phrase meaning the mountains of Megiddo or 'Har-Megiddo.' That translates into the word Armageddon."

I do not see any mountain, but reason that since we look out upon a valley, the vantage point on which we stand can easily be considered the *har.* Even so, would not Har-

Megiddo—literally the mountain of Megiddo—mean a place, not an event?

"No, no," Clyde replies. "This is the site involving all nations. It will be the final battle between the forces of good, led by Christ, and the forces of evil."

Like millions of others, I admit to Clyde, I have always heard of Armageddon. But while often hearing the word, I did not know its derivation. Clyde explains:

"You know we find the word Armageddon only once in the Bible. That, of course, is in the Book of Revelation. That's chapter 16, verse 16." And Clyde quotes the short verse:

"And he gathered them together into a place called in the Hebrew tongue Armageddon."

Since the word Armageddon looms so important in our lives, I hope to pin down its derivation. Still, I am confused. The Old Testament makes no mention of it and Revelation speaks of "a place" called Armageddon. Clyde insists that Armageddon means a battle:

"John the Divine wrote the book of Revelation. And as you know it's from John that we get most of our information on these final days we are passing through. He gives us a perfect picture of this last battle to be fought right here. You recall that in his vision of that great battle he wrote, 'The cities of the nation fell . . . and every island fled away and the mountains were not found.'

Seeing the Signs

You know, I turn back to your ancient prophets in the Old Testament and the signs foretelling Armageddon, and I find myself wondering if we're the generation that's going to see that come about . . . Believe me, (these prophecies) certainly describe the times we're going through.

—President Reagan in a 1983 conversation with Tom Dine of the American Israel Public Affairs Committee

"So God uses John to give us a good description of what this last battle will be like," Clyde continues, quoting scripture about four angels in the river Euphrates, and an army of "two hundred thousand thousand" warriors riding horses breathing "fire and smoke and brimstone."

"This Oriental army, which will be moving westward for one year, will invade and destroy the most populated area of the world before arriving at the River Euphrates.

"Revelation 16 tells us that the River Euphrates will be dry and this will permit the kings of the East, the Orientals, to cross into Israel."

The kings of the East? —I repeat. My mind flits to the area of the world east of the Euphrates. I can call to mind no kings in that area of the world today. In our time, the shah of Iran was the last king east of the Euphrates. There being no kings today—there were kings in John's time—would it not indicate, I suggest, that John was writing for his own age, not ours?

"No, no," says Clyde. "You can take 'kings' to mean leaders, heads of state." A literalist, Clyde, in this instance, does not take the Bible literally. Without my pressing this point, Clyde continues his narrative: "The kings—or leaders—will move the greatest army in the history of the world right here to Megiddo." His eyes enlarge and his face seems to glow as he talks of an angel emptying a vial upon the great river Euphrates and the water drying up, permitting the vast army to march across the riverbed.

"By studying prophecy, one can see that God has fore-told all of these developments. Everything we read that's happening in the world today indicates clearly that this battle will take place very soon.

"And in this final battle—you learn this from studying Zechariah as well as Revelation—the forces of the nations of the entire earth will be fighting against King Jesus and his glorified saints. And as we know, Christ, in history's bloodiest battle, will devastate millions."

To prove his point, Clyde quotes from memory Second Thessalonians 2:8:

"And then shall that Wicked be revealed, whom the Lord shall consume with the spirit of His mouth, and shall destroy with the brightness of His coming."

It is unlikely, I comment to Clyde, that Christians have devoted more thoughts and words to any other place, outside heaven and hell, than to the idea of Armageddon.

As Clyde and I stand talking, others in our group take seats on rocks or on the grass, contemplating the valley with its patchwork fields of wheat, barley and fruit orchards. While it looks quiet and peaceful, Clyde's demeanor and words make the world going up in a big bang appear inevitable. He seems certain of his details and figures regarding a final conflagration.

Yet this battle is to be waged in a field before us, a valley so small it would fit into a Nebraska farm and be lost if placed in a big Texas ranch. Gesturing toward the miniscule quiet valley of terraced fields, I remark to Clyde that it looks very small for the last, great decisive battle.

"Oh, no—it's not too small! You can get a lot of tanks in here."

Tanks, I repeat, and all the armies of the earth?

"All of this. You've got to remember this will be the greatest battle ever fought. Several million will die right here."

Belief in Armageddon

A 1996 Survey of Religion and Politics conducted by the University of Akron revealed that 31 percent of the adult Christian population agree or strongly agree with the belief that the world will end with a battle at Armageddon. This means 62 million Americans accept this belief system.

—University of Akron Professor John Green

And a nuclear war will start here at Megiddo, and destroy the world?

"Yes," he replies. "You read this in Ezekiel, chapters 38 and 39. It describes a nuclear war, saying there will be 'torrential rains and hailstone, fire and brimstone' and 'a great shaking in the land' with mountains falling and cliffs collapsing and walls tumbling to the ground in the face of 'every kind of terror.' Ezekiel could scarcely have been referring to anything other than an exchange of tactical nuclear weapons."

Clyde's certitude staggers my sense of reality. And did Clyde, I ask, visualize Jesus as a five-star general, opting for the use of nuclear weapons?

"Yes," he responds. "In fact, we can expect that Christ will make the first strike. He will release a new weapon. And this weapon will have the same effects as those caused by a neutron bomb. You read that their flesh shall consume away while they stand upon their feet and their eyes shall consume away in their holes, and their tongues shall consume away in their mouths. You see, that's what happens to victims of a thermonuclear blast—so Zechariah had foreknowledge of that."

But is Clyde saying, I ask, that Christ Himself will make the first strike? Before replying, Clyde draws himself up to his full six feet:

"Yes, that's right."

We May Be the Generation That Sees Armageddon

We may be the generation that sees Armageddon.

—President Reagan, speaking in 1980
to Evangelist Jim Bakker

Think of it! At least 200-million soldiers from the Orient, with millions more from the forces of the West . . . of the Revived Roman Empire (Western Europe)! Messiah Jesus will strike those who have ravaged His city Jerusalem. Then He will strike the armies amassed in the valley of Megiddo or Armageddon. No wonder blood will stand to the horses' bridles for a distance of 200 miles from Jerusalem! . . . This whole valley will be filled with war materials, animals, bodies of men, and blood!

It seems incredible! The human mind cannot conceive of such inhumanity of man to man, yet God will allow man's nature to fully display itself in that day. Every city of the world will be destroyed—London, Paris, Tokyo, New York, Los Angeles, Chicago—obliterated!

—Writer Hal Lindsey

3
THE
GOG-MAGOG
WARS

Before the great, final battle of Armageddon, Clyde tells me, we are destined to fight other wars, among them a "Gog-Magog" war.

"You have to distinguish the destruction of Gog from the battle of Armageddon, in which Christ destroys Antichrist's armies. So there's this buildup, terrible years of evil, misery, destruction. You find this in Ezekiel. Ezekiel tells us about the fate of the heathen in the latter days. God is referring not only to Israel's neighbors but more distant enemies as well."

I listen as Clyde quotes Scripture: "And the word of the Lord came unto me, saying 'Son of man, set thy face against Gog.'" "Gog," Clyde insists, "can only mean Russia."

But, I venture to suggest, there was no Russia back in Ezekiel's time.

"But God knew there would be. He had foreknowledge of all that will happen. Now Russia will be totally destroyed. Ezekiel makes this plain. You recall we're told that 'when Gog shall come against the land of Israel' this arouses God's fury. And Ezekiel says that God in His jealousy and with the fire of His wrath will send 'great hailstones, fire and brimstone.' And the 'hail and fire, mixed with blood' of Revelation 8, these," Clyde says, "are modern day missiles."

But why, I ask, in Clyde's theology, must Russia

invade Israel?

"They went against God, with their communism. It was foretold, long ago, they would do this." I listen as Clyde assures me that God in His fury will destroy "five-sixths of the Russian people"—with millions of corpses prey to "ravenous birds of every sort."

So, I ask, Israel is able to lay waste to Gog—that is, the Russian people, as well as destroy Magog, the Russian nation itself?

"Yes—with its allies. Once Russia invades, America and England will go to the aid of Israel. You find this in Daniel 11:30." Clyde cites a verse referring to ships stationed in biblical Chittim. "That's Cyprus, you know, and the British and Americans use that as a base for their fleets, so they can easily go to the aid of Israel. It's not only going to be Russia, but other countries—all those to the north, that invade Israel. This includes the land of Gomer—we know that's modern-day Germany. They will all be destroyed in the period of Tribulation."

"It will be seven years of horrible suffering, of near devastation," Clyde continues. "All of the carnage and destruction, however, is just a prelude, a curtain raiser to the final battle."

I am troubled by his painting Russia and the Russian people as the Number One enemy of Israel, and therefore of God. We're talking peace with the Russians, I point out.

"There will be no peace," Clyde assures me, "until Christ returns—and sits on David's throne."

The Tribulation

An entire country's targets could be hit simultaneously by releasing a SWARM of Cruise missiles—this is a major development in modern warfare, just in time for the tribulation!

—Leon Bates, *Project for Survival*

The Tribulation "will be more catastrophic than the Holocaust...It will be a time of God's revenge upon an unbelieving world...The Tribulation is for Israel.

—Pastor Ken Baugh of the McLean,
Virginia, Bible Church

So the Bible does teach that there will be a nuclear war during the Tribulation? Definitely! A third part of men (will be) killed by the fire and by the smoke, and by the brimstone . . . A fire devoureth before them (Joel 2:3) Who? The northern army—the Russian army—that moves against Israel . . . The whole land shall be devoured by the fire of His jealousy (Zephaniah 1:18). For, behold, the day cometh, that shall burn as an oven (Malachi 4:1). Therefore, both the Old and New Testaments are in agreement concerning a nuclear holocaust.

—TV Evangelist Jack Van Impe

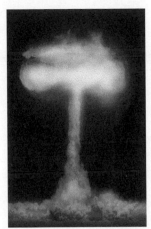

4
WHO IS
THE
ANTICHRIST?

Jerry Falwell on January 15, 1999 told a pastors' conference that the Antichrist—portrayed for some 2,000 years as evil incarnate—may be a Jew alive today. "Of course he'll be Jewish," Falwell told an audience of 1,500 people at a conference on evangelism at Kingsport, Tenn.

"If he's going to be the counterfeit of Christ, he has to be Jewish," Falwell said. "The only thing we know is he must be male and Jewish."

In a note of clarification, made after criticism from Jewish groups, Falwell said, "Since Jesus came to Earth the first time 2,000 years ago as a Jewish male, most evangelicals believe the Antichrist will, by necessity, be a Jewish male."

Falwell is only one in a long list of those who have attempted to pinpoint the identity of the archnemesis of God. It's a deeply held conviction of millions of Christians that there is and always has been an Antichrist.

It was the retired Minneapolis businessman, Clyde, who helped me understand a widely-held view of Antichrist, also known as the Beast.

"The Book of Daniel foretells Antichrist. You recall in Nebuchadnezzar's dream the 'little horn' that sprouts from the Beast. And Daniel tells us about 'the prince that shall come.' And when Daniel speaks of 'the abomination that makes desolate'—we know that means Antichrist's defiling the Temple in Jerusalem.

"In the Book of Revelation—you find this in Chapter 13—a Beast with seven heads and ten horns arises from the sea. He has aspects of a lion, a bear, and a leopard. Then Satan gives the Beast great authority, and enables him to war with the saints, to perform great wonders and gain power 'over all kindred, and tongues, and nations.'"

And, I ask, he takes over during the Tribulation?

"Yes. He will rule during the seven years of the Tribulation. He requires everyone, both small and great, rich and poor, free and bonded, to receive a mark in their right hand, or on their foreheads." Clyde again quotes Scripture:

"Here is the wisdom. Let him that hath understanding count the number of the Beast: for it is the number of a man; and his number is Six hundred threescore and six."

This is where, I say, we get the "mark of the Beast"— and the significance of the numbers 666.

"Yes, even now I believe Antichrist's advance guards are here. They are making this number a component of Antichrist's global system. Look around, you already see these three digits on countless products and financial forms. You see an increasing use of '666' throughout the world.

"You can't imagine Antichrist's ability to gain control," Clyde continues. "He'll be an electrifying, spellbinding speaker. Listeners will be hypnotized by his powers, by his charismatic charms. He'll be using sophisticated surveillance devices. With all of our advanced technology, he'll be seizing control of the world in a way that would have been impossible in any previous generation. First, Antichrist will gain control of ten European nations."

In the beginning, I repeat, it's ten nations?

"You find that in Daniel 7. Daniel tells us of the Beast's ten horns. With the Europeans getting together, we are seeing the fulfillment of prophecy. First, we had the establishment of the Western European Union in 1948 and NATO in 1949 and

Bestowing Values On Current Events

Christian enthrallment with Antichrist is based on "the conviction that total evil can be realized in one individual human and even in a human collectivity." While many societies have beliefs in demonic manifestations, only in Christianity "has the figure of a completely corrupt human agent played so large a role."

The Christian apocalyptic view "bestows value on current events, viewing present conflicts as images or prototypes of the final decisive battle between the forces of good and evil." For some Christians, the Antichrist also is a means of spelling out their own "hatred and fears."

With the split in Western Christianity, the notions of the Antichrist were projected by Catholics and Protestants onto each other. Although the idea of Antichrist has been minimal for Catholics of this century, in Protestantism, Antichrist beliefs have been strong, especially among fundamentalists.

—Bernard McGinn, *Antichrist: Two Thousand Years of the Human Fascination with Evil*

Falwell on Antichrist

Why is the Antichrist leading the armies of the world against Lord Jesus?

Number one, because he hates the sovereignty of God. The battle has always been Satan versus Christ. That's the issue. Secondly, because of the deception of Satan, these nations will come. Third, because of the hatred of the nations for the Lord Jesus Christ.

In John's vision, Lord Jesus Christ is a man sitting on a white horse. And John saw a Beast in his dreams. As Armageddon draws to a close, with millions lying dead, the Lord Jesus will throw the Beast and the false prophet—the Antichrist—into the lake of fire that burns with brimstone.

—TV Evangelist Jerry Falwell

the European Economic Community, or Common Market, in 1957. So this is the reappearance of the Roman Empire in modern form. It's proof the Bible can be trusted. We are witnessing one of the most astonishing and incredible aspects of Bible prophecy!"

So, I say in summary, Antichrist fools *everyone*.

"All the people of the world are taken in by his brilliance, intelligence, his abilities to rule," Clyde continues. "I think he's coming out of Romania. He's a thoroughly evil character."

Is Antichrist the devil? I ask. Or is he a human being?

"One of us, a real human being. He's not synonymous with the devil. That's a spiritual force. Satan aides him. But Antichrist is a completely evil human."

And, I ask, to gain dominance over the earth he first gains control of all the leaders of the world? That, I suggest, must be difficult?

"No, this will be easy. It's easy to explain," he said. "The leaders have geopolitical goals, but they are motivated by 'demonic spirits.' In this case, they are the demonic spirits of the fallen angels who followed Lucifer in his rebellion against God. After these demonic spirits gain control of the minds of the world leaders, these leaders and armies of the world unknowingly become their pawns."

To make sure I am on the right track, I suggest that it will be Antichrist who puts the demonic spirits into the leaders of the world.

Antichrist on TV

Antichrist's announcement of his global destiny will come with "a worldwide press conference televised via satellite."

—TV Evangelist Hilton Sutton

"Yes, that is right," Clyde tells me.

And, having gained control over all the leaders of the world, he naturally has control over all the armies of the world?

"Yes," Clyde assures me. "Antichrist will lead the forces of evil in the final battle, heading up all the armies of the world. We can't imagine the devastation, the suffering. All hell will break loose! All previous wars will seem insignificant. God only knows how tens of millions of people will be wiped out! But they will be *wiped out*. Then God will send Jesus and He will slay Antichrist and, in one hour, destroy all the earth!"

So, the meaning of Antichrist, I ask, is for God to prove He, through His Son, will triumph over evil?

"That's it," Clyde said, reassuringly.

Who Is Antichrist?

▼ In 1530, Martin Luther identified the Pope as Antichrist. John Calvin also made this connection, as did in more recent times the Northern Ireland firebrand Ian Paisley.

▼ In the Middle Ages, some biblical interpreters said Antichrist must be a Muslim, while others named a Jew.

▼ In the 1940s, Hitler frequently was cited, with some saying Gog's ally Gomer, mentioned in Ezekiel 38, referred to Germany.

▼ Mussolini was even more favored, as he ruled in Rome and reportedly intended to revive the Roman Empire.

▼ Stalin often was cited, with texts quoted regarding the evil Gog as being Russia. With the passing years, Gorbachev replaced Stalin.

▼ Saddam Hussein of Iraq is a modern favorite, especially with those who equate Saddam with a former ruler, Nebuchadnezzar and his ancient capital of Babylon.

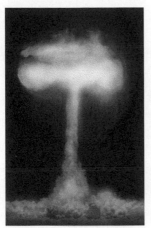

5
WHAT IS THE RAPTURE?

On a Falwell-sponsored tour, I discern that the fundamentalism with which I grew up and the belief system of my traveling companions is different.

Primarily, the Falwell followers hold a different—and a radically new, as history goes—idea about the Rapture.

I credit one of my tour-companions named Brad, age 35, a native of Georgia, unmarried and traveling alone, with helping me understand more about the central role the Rapture plays in his life and in the lives of millions of others who share the same theology.

A financial manager, a person who helps others plan the most profitable way to invest their money, Brad is well-mannered and neatly dressed. Unlike religious zealots who must argue because they cannot discuss, Brad speaks in a soft yet resonant voice. With a full head of red hair and neatly cropped mustache and beard, Brad talks freely of his personal convictions: that in marriage, "the man has to be the boss," and as regards gays, "I think they are sick."

For the most part, our discussions over meals and on long bus rides center on the Bible and Brad's church affiliation, which is Assemblies of God or Pentecostal.

"If you understand prophecy," Brad tells me one day, "you can see how God has divided human history into well-defined time periods. These epochs are called dispensations."

From the time periods, or dispensations, I ask, we get the word dispensationalist?

"I'm proud to say I'm a dispensationalist. Of course Jerry Falwell is—most all of your nationally-known ministers today are. You can't think of many exceptions. For me, I had a hard time understanding the Bible, but now it makes sense. That's because I learned to recognize these time periods.

"We see in each epoch, or dispensation, a progressive order," Brad explains. "All of our understanding of this plan reveals how God deals with humanity.

"God tests us," Brad continues. "In each of the time periods, God tests man for his obedience."

His obedience—to Jesus' commandments? I ask.

"No, these tests relate to man's obedience to some 'dispensation,' some specific revelation of the will of God. They relate with Israel. First, you see, God was expecting the Jews to return 'home.' That was the first step. Second, there had to be an establishment of a Jewish state. And thirdly, we Christians must preach the gospel to all nations, including Israel.

"I expect the fourth event, the Rapture, to occur any day."

Before, I say, the Tribulation? Brad nods his head vigorously, in the affirmative.

But for most all of Christianity, I suggest, clergymen have taught the Rapture would be after the Tribulation.

"The early Christians got it wrong," Brad tells me. "Before the wars and agony engulf the world, Christ will descend and 'snatch away' His true followers. We don't have to die first. Those of us who are Born Again can be free of any worries about the Tribulation, the years of wars, the destruction."

I confess I understand the great appeal of a "*pre*-trib" theology that assures adherents they don't have to stay here for holocausts of the Gog-Magog wars and Armageddon.

Dispensationalism and the Rapture

The Rapture is a key, indispensable ingredient to understanding a new doctrine that emerged as a popular concept in modern fundamentalism less than 200 years ago.

For 1800 years of Christianity, followers of Christ held to the faith that one day He will return. Most read Scripture to say that this will be after a period of great suffering.

Two men largely were responsible for giving a new interpretation to Scripture, called dispensationalism. They said that saved Christians will be Raptured before the Tribulation.

John Darby, a former minister in the Church of England, became an 'apostle and missionary' for this dispensationalist belief. After traveling extensively in Europe, he began missionary journeys in the United States. He met with and influenced leaders of the New Bible and Prophecy Conference movement, which set the tone for the evangelical and fundamentalist movements in North America between 1875 and 1920.

Darby had direct contact with and considerable influence on such evangelical leaders as the Presbyterian James Brookes of Philadelphia; Dwight L. Moody of Chicago; the early evangelical author William E. Blackstone, as well as Cyrus Scofield, who published the Scofield Reference Bible.

Until the mid-1800s and the preaching of Darby and Scofield, no one, whether Catholic or Protestant, had dreamed of an end-time escapism.

Jerry Falwell, Pat Robertson, Jack Van Impe and other dispensationalists appeal to those who long for a certitude that they need not suffer one hour, not one moment of a long period of hardships.

—Dr. James M. Dunn, Baptist Joint Committee, Washington, D.C.

"Yes," Brad agrees. "It's wonderful to know that those of us who are Saved do not have to suffer one moment of agony in the final days."

I also discussed the Rapture with several other Falwell followers, including Clyde, the retired Minneapolis businessman.

"The term Rapture itself is not found in Scripture," Clyde, who apparently has memorized much of the Old and New Testaments, explains. "But it means 'the catching up.' It refers to a scene described in First Thessalonians 4:16-17: 'For the Lord Himself shall descend from heaven with a shout, with the voice of the archangel, and with the trumpet of God. And the dead in Christ shall rise first; then we who are alive and remain shall be caught up together with them in the clouds to meet the Lord in the air.'"

So, I ask Clyde, did he expect his own Rapture might occur at any time?

"That is right. The Rapture can happen anytime. I believe it is the next event. And millions will be caught up."

Didn't his dispensationalist beliefs, I ask, with a pre-tribulation Rapture, entail an extra coming of Christ?

"Yes, in a way. He'll be coming the second time to get his saints. And then of course he'll come back to fight at Armageddon. But you don't have to count the time he comes for the Rapture—he'll perform that in the sky."

And how, I ask, will Christ pick and choose?

Grandstand Seats

Thank God, I will get a view of the Battle of Armageddon from the grandstand seats of the heaven. All who are Born Again will see the Battle of Armageddon, but it will be from the skies.

—Carl McIntire, *Christian Beacon,* June 24, 1965.

"Now in Florida I play golf with a neighbor who has not confessed Jesus Christ as his savior. I witness to him—that Christ can save him from damnation. And I warn him we are approaching the End of Time. We read in First John, 'Children, it is the last hour' . . . And then of course we have the words of Jesus himself, 'Yes, I am coming soon.'

"As an example, I'm driving with my friend who is not Saved, and the Rapture occurs, which, again, I expect any day, and I'm lifted up in the air out of the car. The car runs amok. And my friend is killed in the crash." Clyde, saying he would be Raptured while his friend would not, adds a sentence he likes to repeat, "I rejoice in the idea of meeting my Savior."

Clyde earlier told me his wife had died two years ago. Had she, I ask—and the others in his family—been Saved?

"No, and that bothers me. Neither my wife, before she died, nor my son and his children—none had confessed Christ as their savior. I will be in heaven and I hate to say it, but I will not see them." Clyde speaks of the Saved and unsaved in a quiet voice. He seems certain his God will mete out to most of the dead and the currently alive—all who have not been Born Again—a punishment that will be everlasting.

6
WHO QUALIFIES FOR THE RAPTURE?

If one can escape the suffering of the End Times by being Saved, then being Born Again becomes all important. How does it work?

Generally, if I—or you—say to others, I am Christian, Muslim, Buddhist, Jew, then that makes you one. At least others accept you for your definition. Likewise, we generally think of those who are Saved as those who say they are.

Jerry Falwell says he is. So also does Pat Robertson, Hal Lindsey, Jimmy Swaggart, Thomas D. Ice and all fundamentalist evangelists. Chuck Smith, founding pastor of Cavalry Chapel in Costa Mesa, California, often talks of his being Saved, as does Chuck Missler, a businessman and computer expert; so also does Jack Van Impe of the Trinity Broadcasting Network and James Dobson of Colorado, one of the most widely heard voices in religious broadcasting.

Presidents Jimmy Carter, Ronald Reagan and George Bush alluded to their Born Again experiences. Also Watergate conspirator Charles Colson, exiled Black Panther Party leader Eldridge Cleaver, Hustler magazine publisher Larry Flynt, former Oregon Senator Mark Hatfield, Oliver North, Independent Counsel Kenneth Starr, and many conservative Republican leaders, including Trent Lott and Tom DeLay.

In 1986, 48 percent of southerners described themselves as Born Again Christians, as compared to a slightly lower percentage of Americans in other regions. Those Born Again include all social and economic classes. One poll showed that 50 percent of U.S. college graduates await Jesus Christ's return. Pollsters Gallup and Castelli observed in 1989 that the United States is nearly unique in the Western world with its "unmatched combination of high levels of education and high levels of religious belief and activity."

One of America's most seminal thinkers, William James, wrote in *The Varieties of Religious Experiences* that a "religious experience" that seems to verify a certitude always comes as an individualistic, highly personal revelation. The experience of being Born Again can best be described, perhaps, by personal stories.

My Own Experience:

I grew up in a small, windblown town on the high, dry plains of West Texas. Absorbing biblical terms and concepts as part of my thought process, I was indoctrinated into fundamentalist Christianity. The word of God, I was taught, comes to us through the Bible, free of all mistakes in translations and free of all typographical errors. Every "i" has been dotted and every "t" crossed. I heard repeatedly that the Bible is inerrant, infallible. As a child, I did not know the meaning of the words, but they become lodged deep in my memory.

In the years I was growing up, it was not considered unusual for a man, like my father, to encounter a stranger and without preliminary words of salutation ask, "Are you a Christian? Are you Saved?"

One summer, when I was nine, I visited my maternal grandparents in Arlington. Located between Dallas and Fort Worth, Arlington in that era was a quiet village of so few people that everyone knew everyone else.

A "great revivalist"—as my Grandmother Shanks identified a peripatetic preacher otherwise known as Brother Turner—came to town, put up his tent and preached for a week. Grandmother and I attended every night. Brother Turner preached fire-and-brimstone sermons, telling us that the world is divided into the wicked and the good, the wicked doomed for hell and only the Born Again Christians escaping everlasting fire. "Repent or perish!" he warned.

All of us listening to him were spellbound. Having no radio, television or public cultural events, we depended to a great extent on revivalists such as Brother Turner to bring us knowledge and understanding.

Each night, I experienced a sense of excitement, as well as some dread and growing anticipation. Then came the final night of the revival. Brother Turner held a large Bible in his left hand, quoted directly from God and in conclusion asked those who had not confessed Christ publicly to come forward. Mrs. Triplett, who played the piano, struck the notes for a well-known hymn.

We stood to sing. Grandmother and I held a hymnal, but we knew the words by heart:

> *Just as I am/ without one plea*
> *But that thy blood/ was shed for me*
> *And that thou bidst me/come to Thee*
> *Oh Lamb of God, I come*
> *I come . . .*

No one came forward. Brother Turner asked us to be seated. And he asked Mrs. Triplett to continue playing while we all bowed our heads. After asking those who knew they were Saved to raise their hands, he called on those who had not raised their hands to come forward and be Saved.

Everyone seemed to be thinking of me in those moments. Everyone was softly singing:

> *Just as I am/ and waiting not*
> *To rid my soul/of one dark blot . . .*

Suddenly, as if propelled by forces outside myself, I rose from the wooden bench and moved forward, alone, to where the evangelist was standing. He put his arms around me. And soon my grandmother, neighbors and friends were there to embrace me. I felt myself shaking uncontrollably. Tears were streaming down my face.

Grandmother wrote my parents that I had been Saved. And at summer's end, I returned to Lubbock.

My Father's Experience

As a child, I often heard my father, an early-day cowboy and later cattleman who was on his own at age 13, tell of his conversion, which he recorded in one of his books, *Cowboys and Cattleland*.

"At the age of thirteen something happened to me that has had far-reaching effects on all my after life. Coming home from school as I stepped up on our front porch, a voice told me (not an audible voice, but just the same as if the voice spoke out loud) this message: 'You will be held accountable from this hour forward for all the acts you commit.' Why not voices to me? Socrates said he had voices; he was true to the voices and died for them. John the Baptist said, 'I am but a voice,' and that courageous soul died for the fidelity to the voice. Joan of Arc had voices, and she received for her fidelity to these voices an unfading crown . . . The conviction that came to me at the age of thirteen stayed with me as a warning monitor until the year 1874. During that year I owned a wagon and team, and was hauling freight from Dallas at spare times to make a living.

"While sitting on our front porch one night about 8 p.m., I heard a Methodist preacher exhorting sinners to come to the altar. The meeting was being held under a brush arbor. No one had been talking to me about such things except that silent voice. Then suddenly, conviction came upon me so strong to go to that arbor and altar that I could hardly stand the pressure, but I fought it off.

"I went to bed with my mind made up to hook up the

wagon and team and go to Dallas after freight, trusting that meeting would be over on my return. Having my work on my mind caused the influence to pass off until my return five days later. I arrived home after dark, went to the stables and fed the team, then walked into the kitchen and ate my supper and walked out on the front porch, feeling proud that I had been doing honest work like a man for a good cause. Then I heard the call again; the conviction came with tenfold more power, and I ran for my life, like Pilgrim in Bunyan's *Pilgrim's Progress*, fell at the altar and lay there in awful gloom and despair for two nights, when light broke over my soul, the joy and the dawn of a new day.

"The next day it seemed the sun shone like gold with a halo around it. I loved flowers, people and all Nature as never before . . . There is one thing I know. On that beautiful night, 1874, I passed entirely from Nature's darkness into the marvelous light of a new being."

The Japanese Experience

My father's Born Again experience, and then my own, and similar stories from those I knew, were part of my milieu, episodes I accepted as part of my lifestyle, as real as sun and rain. It was all part of what happened to people, at least the people I knew.

One day I found myself, alone and attempting to make my way as a writer, in Japan. This was soon after World War II. The Japanese were poor, and everyone dressed alike, in what Americans described as black pajama type outfits. Billy Graham came to Tokyo. This was before the Japanese had TV and they knew little about America or Americans, except from having had a nuclear bomb dropped on them and being defeated in the war. They were, however, curious about what we were really like, what we believed—as Americans.

Graham spoke in a huge auditorium, with an interpreter. I was, as far as I could see, the only American in an audience of some 10,000. I looked around me. I saw a mass of people, all with black hair and black eyes and black attire.

Few, if any, until Billy Graham came to Tokyo, had ever heard about being Born Again.

And, unlike my family and friends back in Texas, they were not inclined to get Saved.

I have given the story of my experience and my father's experience to show that this was "our" type of religion. But, as I saw at the Billy Graham crusade in Tokyo, "our" Bible Belt didn't extend to Japan. However, that has changed in recent decades. In our current era, evangelicals, through radio and TV, have invaded most all the corners of the world. According to William Martin, professor of sociology at Rice University, "Fundamentalists and evangelicals (including Pentecostals) constitute about 90 percent of all Protestant missionaries working in foreign lands."

7
BRAD
AND HIS
SCOFIELD
BIBLE

On the Falwell-sponsored Holy Land pilgrimage, I notice each morning when Brad meets our tour bus, he is carrying his Bible, which he identifies for me as a Scofield Reference Bible.

How, I ask one day, when he and I are sitting together, is his Bible different from, say, the King James version?

"Scofield helps us understand passages that might not otherwise be clear," Brad explains. He opens his edition, showing me how Scofield has, in a sense, written his own Bible by inserting his interpretations alongside the biblical text.

Since Brad is a Born Again Christian who believes every word in the Bible is infallible, without error, what about Scofield's words, implanted in a Bible? Might he, I ask, not give them the same authority as the text? Does Brad also accept the notes as infallible?

"Scofield just makes it all crystal clear," Brad says. "Others had predicted the Jews would return to Palestine in the last days, but Scofield saw it was absolutely necessary.

"As Scofield read his Bible, he felt the words he was reading in certain texts were revealing to him certain steps that Christians needed to take in order to hasten the return of Christ. While the words seemed clear to him, he was certain most others might not be as perceptive," Brad explains. "So to spell it out, making the Bible crystal clear about what God required before He could send His Son on a return trip, Scofield thought of inserting his own notes, his own thoughts. This makes it possible for us to understand today's events, in terms of what the Bible has foretold."

So, it's called a reference Bible?

"Yes," Brad says. "And after it was first published in 1909, it became the most widely circulated commentary Bible in all of Christianity. It's been sold in the high multi-million of copies."

Can Brad, I ask, sum up Scofield's thinking?

"He saw all of life, from beginning to the end of eternity. And he saw it all unfolding, in time periods of dispensations."

And he saw *all* the main events centered on a re-created Israel?

"Yes, that's the way it has to be. The Jews must do what they're expected to do—to bring about Christ's return."

And, I ask, after winning—at Armageddon?

"Christ will sit on the throne of King David."

In a Jewish temple?

"Yes. He will rule the world, sitting on King David's throne."

One day, back home in the States, I walked ascending steps to an impressive administration building of the Dallas Theological Seminary. Soon I was seated, by prearrangement, for an interview with the president, Dr. John Walvoord, an impressive man then in his 70s, and proud of his role as mentor to his most famous student, Hal Lindsey.

"God does not look on all of His children the same way," said Walvoord, holding an enormous Bible in one hand.

What, I ask, about the world's one billion Muslims?

God, he tells me, had plans for Jews and Christians, but not for others—unless they became Christians. God, he said, had a heavenly plan for Christians. And an earthly plan for Jews.

And, I ask, the earthly plan for Jews?

"To re-create Israel."

For Walvoord and other Christian fundamentalists, the establishment of Israel in 1948 was a fulfillment of biblical prophecy. They declared this to be a sure sign the clock of biblical prophecy was ticking and that we were rapidly approaching the final events leading to the return of Jesus.

Many Christians who grew up with dispensationalism have evolved, they say, to realize the doctrine is not "Christian." Dale Crowley Jr., a religious broadcaster in Washington, D.C., is an example. I have known Crowley and his wife Mary for a couple of decades. We share kindred spirits that we trace back to early days in Texas, as well as our memories of days in Japan, when he was a missionary there and I was a journalist living in Tokyo. Crowley was especially helpful to me in understanding aspects of my research for an earlier book, *Prophecy and Politics*.

He told me that in his youth he had accepted the Scofield doctrine.

"Yes, I grew up with dispensationalism. I vividly recall at age 18, with my own earnings, buying a Scofield Bible. I was taught dispensationalism by scores of Sunday School teachers, pastors, evangelists, Bible conference speakers, as well as a college professor, for whom I held the deepest admiration.

"I pastored, preached, taught and evangelized with this doctrine until one day I sat down with Dr. James R. Graham, a China missionary, educator and theologian. The year was 1952. Taking my Scofield Bible in hand, Dr. Graham got right down to business, point by point, step by step, demolishing every tenet in the dispensational house of cards.

"First, he explained it was a new system of prophetic interpretation—then only 120 years old. This means that for 1800 years the church of Jesus Christ did not hold such views as you read in Scofield. Christianity, in other words, survived very well without this new, strange and dangerous doctrine."

Dr. Graham, who served on Billy Graham's board of directors, but was not related, "opened my eyes," Crowley said, to these fallacies:

▼ Scofield's system of biblical interpretation destroys the unity of the Bible, particularly the unity of God's love and grace to mankind for all ages.

▼ It violates the meaning of Christ—and Christianity.

▼ It does so by making Christians hostages to what present-day Jews do—or don't do.

▼ Scofield's dispensationalism places not Christ but rather Jews—and Israel—on center stage. Holding that the Jewish state has first priority with God, the doctrine makes a cult of the land of Israel. It places the Jewish state—and its priority with God—above the Church and the teaching of its head, Jesus Christ.

▼ Scofield's dispensationalism not only holds Christ and Christianity in hostage, but also God. It teaches that God cannot permit Christ to return until the Jews do their "earthly" part in a Scofield-devised scenario.

▼ Scofield taught that "God has earthly promises for His earthly elect"— the Jews, and "heavenly promises for His heavenly elect"—the Christians. That is pure Scofield. But it's not to be found in Holy Scripture.

▼ Scofield's dispensationalism cites "unconditional" covenants between God and man. But there is not one unconditional covenant in all Scripture.

▼ Scofield's dispensationalism negates the doctrine of the New Covenant established between God and all mankind by the blood of the crucified, buried and risen Christ.

▼ Scofield's dispensationalism teaches a "secret" Rapture. The word, from the Greek meaning "snatching away," is subjective, not the objective reality. The major event is the Resurrection. The so-called Rapture is a minor event. Scofield's dispensationalism makes it a major event.

▼ Scofield's dispensationalism teaches that Christ will return to establish a Jewish kingdom, sitting on a throne in the third temple in Jerusalem, and presiding over Old Testament style temple worship such as sacrifices of red heifers. Reverting to tribal laws was not, Dr. Graham reminded me, what Christ was about. He came with a new message. And He is now sitting on an eternal throne. He is the eternal King ruling over an eternal kingdom. His mission was fulfilled.

Why, I asked Crowley, did he think dispensationalism had gained so many adherents?

"It appeals to those who like to feel they are on the 'inside,' that they are getting 'the news' in advance, that they and others like them know what was always in the mind of God.

"Charismatic ministers tell their followers if they accept a cult of the land of Israel and the epochs or dispensations that must transpire there, they will join an 'in' crowd and be rewarded with power, order, security and personal meaning."

Growing Numbers

There are probably 80,000 Fundamentalist pastors in the U.S., many of whom broadcast on 1,000 Christian radio stations and 100 Christian television stations— and the vast majority of these are dispensationalists.

In short, most all of the TV and radio preachers today are propagating Scofield's doctrine. Dispensationalists represent about 15 to 20 percent of the 15 million member Southern Baptist Convention. They also represent some 15 to 20 percent of all Pentecostal and charismatic Christians. Altogether I estimate they number 25 to 30 million. And they are growing.

Large and influential seminaries that teach dispensationalism include the Dallas Theological Seminary, where Hal Lindsey studied, as well as the Moody Bible Institute of Chicago, the Philadelphia College of the Bible, the Bible Institute of Los Angeles, and about 200 other colleges and institutes.

In 1998, there were more than 100,000 students in Bible schools and eighty to ninety percent of the teachers as well as their students are dispensationalists.

These Bible college graduates will go out, become ministers and preach Scofield dispensationalism in their churches, or they will start their own Bible schools and teach it.

Of the 4,000 Evangelical-Fundamentalists who attend the National Religious Broadcasters convention annually, at least 3,000 are dispensationalists who accept as certitude that a cataclysm lies ahead—but they won't suffer one moment of agony due to their early Rapture.

—Dale Crowley Jr., religious broadcaster, Washington, D.C.

The Scofield Bible

The various millennial currents were most effectively solidified in the Scofield Bible . . . . The significance of the Scofield Bible cannot be overestimated.

—Dwight Wilson, *Armageddon Now!*

Scofield had an enormous impact on selling dispensationalism by implanting his own ideas in the Bible. This meant that many in the pew failed to distinguish between the words of Scofield and those of the Holy Spirit.

—Joseph M. Canfield, *The Incredible Scofield and His Book*

Cyrus Scofield: 1843-1921

A Tennessean dogged by scandal, heavy drinking, and marital problems in his early years, Scofield fought as a Confederate in the Civil War, practiced law in Kansas, and hastily left that state in 1877 (abandoning a wife and two children) amid accusations that he had stolen political contributions to Senator John Ingalls, a former partner. (No one who knew Scofield's early life, Ingalls later observed, could "doubt the efficacy of the scheme of Christian salvation.")

Jailed in St. Louis in 1879 on forgery charges, Scofield experienced religious conversion in prison and fell under the influence of James Brookes, the Darbyite dispensationalist. In 1882 he became pastor of Dallas' First Congregational Church . . .

Scofield's continuing reputation rests on his Reference Bible (1909) . . . One scholar has called it "perhaps the most important single document in all fundamentalist literature."

—Paul Boyer, *When Time Shall Be No More*

JERUSALEM–CENTER STAGE

8

JERUSALEM
IN
HISTORY

Except for stories I'd heard in my childhood Sunday School, I knew little or nothing about a Jerusalem where people live everyday lives—where they are born, go to school, get married, have children, at times laugh and celebrate, at other moments cry and mourn. Then, one day, moving to Jerusalem, I began to experience the realities of a people who have always lived there.

I walk the cobblestone streets with an Arab Muslim, Mahmud Ali Hassan, who was born in Jerusalem, bought his first pair of shoes, got his first shave from a barber, was fitted for his first suit of clothes, was married, saw all his children born and watched them grow up—all in the Old Walled City.

With Mahmud, I walk along narrow corridors within one of the few remaining examples in the world of a completely walled town. The walls stand partially on the foundation of Hadrian's Square, built in A.D. 135. They include remains of earlier walls, those of King Herod in 37 B.C., and Agrippa, A.D. 41, and Saladin, 1187. And finally the walls were rebuilt by the Turkish Muslim, Suleiman the Magnificent, in the sixteenth century.

"This Old Walled City throughout its long history has been predominantly inhabited by Arabs," Mahmud tells me. "And Arab markets, Arab homes and Arab religious sites make up about ninety percent of the Old City.

"As Arabs, we are descendants of an indigenous people, a people who never left Palestine, continually having lived within these old walls," Mahmud continues. "I can trace my forebears back more than ten generations. And in the case of my father and his father and his father, our families have lived in the same house for the past three hundred years."

Mahmud and I approach the Muslim Noble Sanctuary or Haram al-Sharif.

It is a Friday, a Muslim Holy Day, and walking toward the mosque called Al-Aqsa, we move among thousands of Arabs as they make their way along Jerusalem's cobblestone corridors to pray.

"This is one of the oldest cities in the world," Mahmud reminds me. "Arabs called Amorites came here four to five thousand years ago. They established this site as a religious foundation to honor their god. And these early Arab worshipers of a god they called Shalem gave us the name of our Holy City, Jerusalem. Then came others of our forebears, the Canaanites from Canaan. They made Jerusalem an early center of worship of the One God. The Canaanites had a king named Melchizedek, and it is written that he also was a priest of God Most High.

"All this early history predates the arrival of the Hebrews by many centuries," Mahmud continues. "And when a tribe of Hebrews, one of many tribes in the area, did arrive, they stayed for less than 400 years. And they, too, like many before and after, were defeated. And 2,000 years ago they were driven out."

From Al-Aqsa, we walk a short distance toward the magnificent Dome of the Rock, one of the most beautiful shrines in all the world—often compared in its beauty with the Taj Mahal. "It was constructed in 685," Mahmud tells me, "by the order of Abdul-Malek Ibn Marwan."

I've been told, I say to Mahmud, this is the Mosque of Omar.

"Everyone nowadays, even the Muslims, refer to this as the Mosque of Omar, but Omar didn't build it. Rather, the

Umayyad Caliph of Damascus."

To visit the shrine, an octagonal masterpiece fashioned with blue and green tiles that glisten in the Mediterranean light, we step onto a raised, terrace-like platform, surrounded by pillars with stairways on every side. We look above to an incredibly large yet graceful dome.

At the entrance, we, along with dozens of other visitors from around the world, remove our shoes and once inside walk on ancient, richly textured Oriental rugs. After some half-dozen steps we reach a guardrail framing a large boulder. I am startled by the unexpected dimensions of the rock. The rock, which rises above the ground to my shoulders and covers an area half the size of a tennis court, dominates the entire space within the shrine.

Jerusalem's most beautiful architectural gem was built for one sole purpose: to protect and enhance the huge rock, Mahmud relates. "Our prophet Muhammad believed this great rock had its origins in Paradise. And it was from this sacred rock that Muhammad was transported by God to heaven."

It is a short walk back to the convent within the Old City where I am living. Mahmud accompanies me. Along the way, Mahmud tells me:

"As Arabs, as Muslims, our quarrel has never been with Jews as Jews, or with the great religion of Judaism. The places that the Jews and Christians revere as holy, we revere as holy. The prophets the Jews and Christians revere as holy, we revere as holy. My point," Mahmud concludes, "is that everyone in history has borrowed from what went before. No one or no one group has exclusive rights here. There were countless battles over Jerusalem. And the Hebrews were in power here only sixty years."

I confess to Mahmud that I am a typical American: I never really studied the history of Jerusalem and Palestine. Like most all Western Protestants, I had as a frame of reference only the biblical stories, written or recorded millennia ago.

I had the old biblical stories and the news of the day,

in which Israeli Jews claimed they had exclusive rights, in perpetuity, to Jerusalem.

Mahmud didn't fit into those myths about a land for only one group of people. And this was disconcerting.

9
INVISIBLE
CHRISTIANS

On Falwell-sponsored tours, I was one of more than 600 Christians on the first excursion in 1983, and on a second trip in 1985 I was one of more than 800 Christians. In colored brochures outlining each trip, Falwell did not mention we would be in the Land of Christ, where Jesus was born, had his ministry and died. Rather, the focus was on Israel. We had only Israeli guides, stayed only in Israeli hotels and ate only in Israeli restaurants.

Christians were all around us, tens of thousands of them. But Falwell did not arrange for us to meet Christians.

One day, I skip a visit to an Israeli military site to visit with Jonathan Kuttab, a Palestinian Christian. I locate his law offices, a short walking distance from the American Colony Hotel in Arab East Jerusalem. Soon, I'm seated across his desk, drinking Arab coffee.

Born in Jerusalem, educated in the United States, where he received his law degree, Kuttab has long researched the history of Christianity. He is often a participant in inter-faith conferences in Washington, D.C., as well as in Jerusalem.

Why, in his opinion, I ask, does Falwell bring hundreds of American tourists to the Land of Christ—and not meet a Christian?

"He takes them to see stone monuments—but ignores

'the Living Stones,' the Christians who have kept Christianity alive in the land where it was born. We've been here since the days of Christ. Yet, he makes us, the indigenous Christians, *not here,* invisible."

In his research, when was it, I ask, that Western Christians began doing this? "This began after the Reformation. Prior to that, the traditional Catholic thought was that this was the Holy Land of Jesus Christ. The teachings up to that time did not include the possibility of Jews returning to Palestine, nor any concept of a Chosen People or a concept of the existence of a Jewish nation," Kuttab said.

"Christian leaders originally all agreed that the prophecies regarding a Jewish Restoration applied to the return of the Israelites from exile in Babylon. You'll recall that, in the 6th century BC, the ruler Cyrus allowed the Jews, who had been driven out of Palestine, to return. With that, Christian leaders said the prophecies of Jews returning to Palestine had been fulfilled.

"So, until the 1600s," Kuttab continues, "it was taught that the Christian Church became the direct heir to the Hebrew religion. Thus, no one was looking upon the Jews as the Chosen People destined to return to Palestine. In Christianity, no one felt a romantic affection for the ancient glories of Hebrew warriors."

Then, I suggest, Christians were rather unanimous in agreeing that in their religion of Christianity, Christ superseded, that is, replaced the old Hebraic traditions?

"St. Augustine in his *City of God* and other works makes this plain—that the Christian Church embodies the millennial kingdom of God," Kuttab says. "He was writing back in the 5th century. And, of course, he's still widely appreciated and read today."

If, I ask, Christ embodies the millennial kingdom, why did so many Christians take a different slant—beginning with the Reformation?

"Until that time, the Old Testament had not been translated into the vernacular. After the 1600s, it became widely

Israel as Prophecy

The creation of Israel in 1948 means "a return at last, to the biblical land from which the Jews were driven so many hundreds of years ago . . . The establishment of the nation of Israel is the fulfillment of biblical prophecy and the very essence of its fulfillment."

—Former President Jimmy Carter

As a Christian, I see the return of Jews to the Holy Land but one sign of the coming of the messianic age in which all humans will enjoy the benefits of an ideal society.

—Former Senator Mark Hatfield

For the first time in more than 2,000 years, Jerusalem, being in the hands of the Jews, gives the student of the Bible a thrill and a renewed faith in the accuracy and validity of the Bible.

—L. Nelson Bell, 1967, editor, *Christianity Today,* on the occasion of Israeli troops capturing Jerusalem

During the Reformation era the Biblical Hebrews came to be associated with their modern co-religionists. At the same time it became popular belief among Protestant adherents that the Jews scattered in their present dispersion would be regathered in Palestine in order to prepare for the Second Coming of Christ . . . The Old Testament not only became the most popular literature for the Protestant laity, but also the source book for general historical knowledge. This is the moment when a process of historical manipulation began.

—Regina Sharif, *Non-Jewish Zionism*

available and interpreted by individual readers. With this change, we had a 'Hebraic' or 'Judaizing' revival. Instead of Christ's simple teachings, Christian ministers turned to Old Testament war stories, to Abraham, Isaac and Jacob.

"Moreover, Christians began making the Hebrew Bible their only reference to history. They became intensely occupied with the world to come. They began to view life as having an imminent ending. They turned to messianism and millenarianism, both features of the Judaic tradition."

Kuttab repeats what the Muslim Mahmud had earlier told me, that as a Palestinian he belongs to ancient people who settled and lived in Palestine for much longer periods than the Hebrews. "Yet Christian fundamentalists somehow skip 2,000 years and reduce the total history of Palestine to only the Jewish presence here.

"This means that Falwell and his followers, who base their Christianity on Old Testament stories of a Chosen Land for a Chosen People, pretend we are not here. They adopt a racist doctrine that makes us invisible," Kuttab concludes. "We don't fit into their Hebraic scenario."

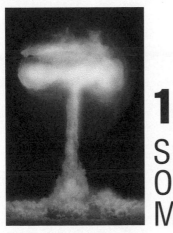

10
SIEGE
ON A
MOSQUE

In early 1999, members of a Denver, Colorado dispensationalist group called Concerned Christians were arrested by Israeli police, handcuffed, jailed as common criminals and deported back to the States. Israeli police accused them of planning a "bloody apocalypse" to hasten the Second Coming of Christ. It was suggested that they plotted the destruction of Jerusalem's most holy Islamic shrine.

In a fervent wish to replace the mosque with a Jewish temple, the Denver cult members are no different from other dispensationalists who believe God wants this done. As I learned from Christians on a Falwell-sponsored tour, they hold this idea quite sacred. A retired Army major named Owen, who lives in northern Nebraska, seems typical.

I spent much time with Owen, a widower, who is slightly built and about five feet, five inches tall. He stands erect and has a pleasant smile. Well dressed and with a full head of sandy hair, he looks younger than his age. He had served in Europe during World War II and later for a number of years in Japan.

One day, as I am walking alongside Owen, our group moves toward the old walled city. As we enter Damascus Gate and pass along cobblestone corridors, I easily imagine Jesus having walked a similar route. In the midst of a rapidly changing environment, the old walled city, guarding layer upon layer of history and conflict, provides the stellar attraction for tourists and remains home for 25,000 people. As the Palestinian Muslim Mahmud had told me earlier, throughout its long history, Jerusalem has been predominantly and overwhelmingly Arab.

We approach Haram al-Sharif, or Noble Sanctuary, which encloses the Dome of the Rock and Al-Aqsa Mosque—sites which I had visited earlier with Mahmud. Both these edifices, on raised platform grounds, generally are called simply "the mosque" and represent Jerusalem's most holy Islamic shrine.

We stand on lower ground below the mosque and face the Western Wall, a 200-foot-high and 1,600-foot-long block of huge white stones, believed to be the only remnant of the second Jewish temple.

"There—"our guide said, pointing upward toward the Dome of the Rock and Al-Aqsa mosque—"we will build our Third Temple. We have all the plans drawn for the temple. Even the building materials are ready. They are hidden in a secret place. There are several shops where Israelis work, making the artifacts we will use in the new temple. One Israeli is weaving the pure linen that will be used for garments of the priests of the temple." He pauses, then adds:

"In a religious school called Yeshiva Ateret Cohanim— the Crown of the Priests—located near where we are standing, rabbis are teaching young men how to make animal sacrifice."

A woman in our group, Mary Lou, a computer specialist, seems startled to hear the Israelis want to return to the rites of the old Solomonic sacrificial altar of the temple.

"You are going back to animal sacrifice?" she asks. "Why?"

"It was done in the First and Second Temples," our Israeli guide says. "And we do not wish to change the practices. Our sages teach that neglecting to study the details of temple service is a sin."

Leaving the site, I remark to Owen that our Israeli guide had said a temple must be rebuilt on the Dome of the Rock site. But he said nothing about the Muslim shrines.

"They will be destroyed," Owen tells me. "You know it's in the Bible that the temple must be rebuilt. And there's no other place for it except on that one area. You find that in the law of Moses."

Did it seem possible, I ask Owen, that the Scripture about building a temple would relate to the time in which it was written—rather than to events in the the current era?

"No, it is related to our era," Owen says. "The Bible tells us that in the End Times the Jews will have renewed their animal sacrifice."

In other words, I repeat, a temple must be built so that the Jews can resume their animal sacrifice?

"Yes," said Owen, quoting Ezekiel 44:29 to prove his point.

Is Owen convinced that Jews, aided by Christians, should destroy the mosque, build a temple and reinstate the killing of animals in the temple—all in order to please God?

"Yes," he replies. "That's the way it has to be. It's in the Bible."

And does the building of the temple, I ask, fit into any time sequence?

Red Heifers

The Rev. Clyde Lott, Canton, Miss., a Pentecostal minister, interprets passages of the Bible to say that a third Jewish temple must rise in Jerusalem before the Second Coming can happen . . . Lott is producing perfect red heifers, virginal cows "without spot" that could be sacrificed to produce ashes for ritual use in the future temple. For that to happen, Muslim shrines like the Dome of the Rock would have to be knocked down . . .

(Lott is) convinced that God will attend to this in due time.

—*The New York Times,* December 27, 1998.

"Yes. We think it will be the next step in the events leading to the return of our Lord. As far as its being a large temple, the Bible doesn't tell us that. All it tells us is that there will be a renewal of sacrifices. And Jews can do that in a relatively small building."

Isn't it atavistic, I ask, to go back to animal sacrifice? And what about a multitude concerned with animal rights in our modern age?

"But we don't care what they say. It's what the Bible says that's important," Owen stresses. "The Bible predicts a rebuilding of a temple. Now the people who are going to do it are not Christians but Orthodox Jews. Of course the Old Testament made out a very specific formula for what the Jews must follow regarding animal sacrifice. They can't carry it out without a temple. They were observing animal sacrifice until 70 A.D. And when they have a temple they will have some Orthodox Jews who will kill the sheep or oxen in the temple, as a sacrifice to God."

As Owen talks of reinstating animal sacrifice—a step he feels necessary for his own spiritual maturity—he seems to block from his awareness the fact that Muslim shrines stand on the site where he says God *demands* a temple be built.

That evening, after dinner, Owen and I take a long walk. Again, I voice my concerns about the dangers inherent in a plot to destroy Islam's holy shrines.

"Christians need not do it," Owen says, repeating what he told me earlier. "But I am sure the shrines will be destroyed."

But, I insist, this can well trigger World War III.

"Yes, that's right. We are near the End Times, as I have said. Orthodox Jews will blow up the mosque and this will provoke the Muslim world. It will be a cataclysmic holy war with Israel. This will force the Messiah to intervene." Owen speaks as calmly, as softly as if telling me there'd be rain tomorrow.

"Yes," he adds, as we return to our hotel. "There definitely must be a third temple."

Back home in Washington, D.C.—after going on the first Falwell-sponsored tour and meeting Owen—I talked with Terry Reisenhoover, a native of Oklahoma, who told me he raised money to help Jewish terrorists destroy the Muslim shrines.

Reisenhoover—short, rotund, balding and a Born Again Christian blessed with a fine tenor voice— told me he frequently was invited during the Reagan administration to White House gatherings of dispensationalists, where he was a featured soloist.

Reisenhoover spoke freely to me of his plans to move tax-free dollars from American donors to Israel. In 1985 he served as chairman of the American Forum for Jewish-Christian Cooperation, being assisted by Douglas Krieger as executive director, and an American rabbi, David Ben-Ami, closely linked with Ariel Sharon.

Additionally, Reisenhoover served as chairman of the board for the Jerusalem Temple Foundation, which has as its sole purpose the rebuilding of a temple on the site of the present Muslim shrine. Reisenhoover chose as the foundation's international secretary Stanley Goldfoot. Goldfoot emigrated in the 1930s from South Africa to Palestine and became a member of the notorious Stern gang, which shocked the world with its massacres of Arab men, women and children. Such figures as David Ben-Gurion denounced the gang as Nazis and outlawed them.

Goldfoot, according to the Israeli newspaper *Davar,* placed a bomb on July 22, 1946, in Jerusalem's King David Hotel that destroyed a wing of the hotel housing the British Mandate secretariat and part of the military headquarters. The operation killed some 100 British and other officials and, as the Jewish militants planned, hastened the day the British left Palestine.

"He's a very solid, legitimate terrorist," Reisenhoover said admiringly of Goldfoot. "He has the qualifications for clearing a site for the temple."

Reisenhoover also said that while Christian militants

are acting on religious fervor, their cohort Goldfoot does not believe in God or sacred aspects of the Old Testament. For Goldfoot, it's a matter of Israeli control over all of Palestine.

"It is all a matter of sovereignty," Goldfoot deputy Yisrael Meida, a member of the ultra right-wing Tehiya party, explained. "He who controls the Temple Mount, controls Jerusalem. And he who controls Jerusalem, controls the land of Israel."

Reisenhoover told me he had sponsored Goldfoot on several trips to the United States, where Goldfoot spoke on religious radio and TV stations and to church congregations. Reisenhoover helped me secure a tape cassette of a talk Goldfoot made in Chuck Smith's Calvary Chapel in Costa Mesa, California. In soliciting donations for a temple, Goldfoot did not tell the Christians about plans to destroy the mosque.

Reisenhoover had given me several names of persons who knew Stanley Goldfoot, among them George Giacumakis, who for many years headed the Institute for Holy Land Studies, a long established American-run evangelical school for studies in archaeology and theology. On one of my visits to Jerusalem, I made an appointment with Giacumakis, a Greek American with dark eyes and cultivated charm.

Might he, I asked, after we had visited casually over coffee, help me arrange an interview with Goldfoot?

"Oh, no," Giacumakis responded, dropping his head into both hands, as one does on hearing a disaster. "You don't want to meet him. He goes back to the Irgun terrorist group!" Raising his head and waving an arm toward the King David Hotel, he added, "Stanley Goldfoot was in charge of that operation. He will not stop at anything. His idea is to rebuild the temple, and if that means violence, then he will not hesitate to use violence."

Giacumakis paused, then assured me that while he himself did not believe in violence, "If they do destroy the mosque and the temple is there, that does not mean I will not support it."

It was also Terry Reisenhoover who helped me get acquainted with the Reverend James E. DeLoach, a leading figure in the huge Second Baptist Church of Houston. After we had talked a few times on the telephone, DeLoach volunteered he would be in Washington, D.C. He came by my apartment, at my invitation, and I set my tape recording running—with his permission.

"I know Stanley very very well. We're good friends," he said. "He's a very strong person."

Of Reisenhoover, DeLoach said, "He's very talented—at raising money. He's raising $100 million. A lot of this has gone to paying lawyers who gained freedom for 29 Israelis who attempted to destroy the mosque. It cost us quite a lot of money to get their freedom."

And how, I ask, did he and the others funnel the money from U.S. donors to the aid of the Jewish terrorists?

"We've provided support for the Ateret Cohanim Yeshiva."

The Jewish school, I asked, that prepares students to make animal sacrifice?

"Yes," he agreed.

And Christian donors are paying for that?

"It takes a lot of training," he said. Then, quite proudly: "I've just hosted in my Houston home two fine young Israelis who study how to do the animal sacrifice in the temple to be built."

The Building of The Temple Is Near

A late 1998 Israeli newsletter posted on a "Voice of the Temple Mount" Web site says its goal is "the liberation" of the Muslim shrines and the building on that site of a Jewish Temple.

"Now the time is ripe for the Temple to be rebuilt," says the Israeli newsletter.

The newsletter calls upon "the Israeli government to end the pagan Islamic occupation" of lands where the mosque stands. It adds, "The building of the Third Temple is near."

Pastor DeLoach talked for more than one hour, all of which he permitted me to record.

Before he left my apartment, I asked one final question: what if the Jewish terrorists he supports are successful and they destroy the Dome of the Rock and Al-Aqsa—shrines holy to every fifth person in the world today—and this triggers World War III and a nuclear holocaust? Would he and Reisenhoover not be responsible?

"No," he said—because what they are doing is "God's will."

It was Pastor DeLoach who suggested I get in touch with Dr. Lambert Dolphin, a top-ranking scientist with the Stanford Research Institute in California. The Houston pastor said Dolphin was "x-raying" the mosque grounds, in preparation for the building of a temple. "He is the innovator of a plan that uses ground search radar sort of like an x-ray machine for archaeological purposes. His ground search radar has a great deal of validity."

I began a correspondence with Dr. Dolphin. He sent large packages with explanations on "ground search radar" as well as a pamphlet describing his personal life and his having undergone a Born Again experience. Finding Christ in his case also meant accepting the dispensationalists' belief that God wants a Jewish temple built before He can send Christ back to earth.

His "Geophysical Methods for Archaeological Surveys in Israel" describes how an area can be explored archaeologically by aerial photography, thermal infrared imagery, ground penetration radar and seismic sounding—without actual digging.

In another pamphlet, Dolphin notes that on the Islamic holy grounds, "Digging is difficult and remote sensing is to be preferred." In asking for funds—to be sent to Stanley Goldfoot—Dolphin gives a cost estimate of "low six figures to mid-seven figures" for a single field season.

On a mission authorized by the Jerusalem Temple Foundation and partially funded by Chuck Smith's Calvary

Chapel, Dr. Dolphin spent several weeks at the Muslim site with staff and electronic devices. However, after much "x-raying" of the grounds of the Dome of the Rock and Al-Aqsa mosque, Dolphin raised the ire of Muslims, who voiced strenuous objections to his being there. Dolphin packed his gear and returned to California. As of 1999, he remains a fervent dispensationalist, and continues to plan the elimination of the mosque and the building of a Jewish Temple. He has his own Web site to inform readers of the progress.

Since 1967—the year the Israelis seized military control of Jerusalem—militant Jews, many of them armed Israeli rabbis, officers, soldiers and religious students, have on more than 100 occasions stormed Jerusalem's most holy Islamic grounds. Shlomo Goren, who later became Israel's chief rabbi, was one of the first. In August 1967, he led 50 armed militants onto the site.

As of 1999, Israeli chief rabbis had never, in more than three decades of terrorist attacks on the mosque, condemned the Jewish militants. The lack of condemnation, said one Israeli journalist, indicates that the highest Israeli officials sanction the actions of the terrorists. "The chief rabbis, who receive their salaries from the state, haven't condemned at all the violence committed," the journalist noted, adding that their lack of condemnation signaled the government's complicity.

In most armed assaults on Haram al-Sharif, it's been militant rabbis who were instigators and leaders. "We should not forget," said Rabbi Shlomo Chaim Hacohen Aviner, "that the supreme purpose of the ingathering of exiles and the establishment of our state is the building of the temple. The temple is the very top of the pyramid."

I first heard of militant Jewish plans to destroy the mosque in 1979. In that year, I went to occupied Palestine (the West Bank) and stayed in the homes of Jewish settlers who call themselves the Bloc of the Faithful, or Gush Emunim. They were there in violation of all international laws that forbid occupation of land taken by force of arms. I found myself living in strange ghettos, protected by high barbed wire fences, search beams and armed sentries.

About one-third of the settlers I met were from the States, most of them from New York. Bobby Brown from Brooklyn was typical. "If destroying the mosque to build a temple creates a big war, then so be it," he told me. He, like all the others around me, carried Israeli army-issued submachine guns.

"We feel it is a stain on our land to have a mosque sitting in our midst," Brown, a third-generation American, continued, speaking from a settlement called Tekoa on the outskirts of Bethlehem. "You look at any picture of Jerusalem and you see that mosque! That will have to go. One day we will build our Third Temple there. We must do this to show the Arabs, and all the world, that we Jews have sovereignty over all of Jerusalem, over all the Land of Israel."

I stayed in the home of Linda and Bobby Brown. One evening I suggest that to build a temple—by destroying the mosque—could ignite an apocalyptic war. "Exactly," said Brown. "But we want that kind of war—because we *will* win it. We will then expel all of the Arabs from the Land of Israel. And," he emphasized, "we will rebuild our temple."

Even as he spoke, Gush Emunim militants were meeting secretly to plot destruction of the mosque. As was later documented, they obtained aerial photos of the mosque and recruited an air force pilot to steal a plane and strafe it. Then, they opted for a ground attack.

"Squads of bomb-laden Jews were to scale the Old City walls into the mosque's courtyard," Robert I. Friedman reported in a 1985 issue of *The Village Voice*. "A model of the mosque was built, practice runs were timed; homemade explosives were tested in the desert." Menachem Livni, a bearded, stern-faced commander of a reserve battalion of combat engineers in the Israeli army, "calculated which way the mosque would fall after it exploded and how far the shrapnel would be catapulted."

Before they could carry out their plot, however, they were arrested. At a trial, they were treated as great heroes. One of the terrorists, Yehuda Etzion, told the court that because the Israeli government itself would not "purify" the Muslim site, he realized "I myself must do it." He was not repentant: "I'm 100 percent innocent," he told the court, "because the building (Dome of the Rock) will be removed."

None of the militants served long sentences. The President of Israel commuted their prison sentences. The militants had plenty in defense funds, with dollars flowing in from the United States from both Christians and Jews.

The U.S. Treasury provides the largest source of funding for the Gush Emunim and their illegal West Bank and East Jerusalem settlements. Hundreds of millions of taxpayers' dollars have been funneled into building the illegal Jewish settlements and their costly infrastructure.

"There Remains But One More Event . . ."

There remains but one more event to completely set the stage for Israel's part in the last great act of her historical drama. This is to rebuild the ancient Temple of worship upon its old site. There is only one place that this Temple can be built, according to the law of Moses. This is upon Mt. Moriah. It is there that the two previous Temples were built.

—Hal Lindsey, *The Late Great Planet Earth*

THE CHRISTIAN RIGHT—ISRAEL AND AMERICAN JEWS

11
THE CHRISTIAN RIGHT–AND ANTI-SEMITISM

The Christian church throughout most of its history "has been anti-Semitic," retired Duke Divinity School professor O. Kelly Ingram writes in his study, "The Roots of Christian Anti-Semitism." Published in a November, 1983, *Link*, his article points out that for about 1,700 years the Church practiced an avowed hatred, based largely on theological issues.

The anti-Semitism was especially strident during the first 300 years of the Christian era when the "Christian church and the Jewish religious community were rivals." To prove this point, he turns to several early Church leaders:

▼ Justin Martyr, approving the destruction of Israel and quoting from Isaiah, wrote Jews were rightly suffering: "Your country is desolate, your cities are burned with fire, your land, strangers devour it in your presence."

▼ Tertullian spoke of the Jews with undisguised hatred. As their punishment, he said their temple and country were in ruins and the people dispersed the world over.

▼ Hippolytus of Rome accused the Jews of participating in the persecution of Christians.

▼ Eusebius of Caeserea in his *Ecclesiastical History* wrote that the Old Testament prophecies had been fulfilled in Jesus and power and leadership in Israel had come into the hands of the Christian Messiah. "The historic world mission of the people of Israel has been taken from them and has been given to the Christian churches."

▼ After 300 years struggling for its existence, Christianity, Ingram reports, "turned from a persecuted sect into a power that both persecuted and afflicted others." Church leaders joined by Christian emperors sought to prevent Jews from mingling with Christians. In the words of British historian Cecil Roth, Christians drove Jews "out of ordinary activities, and restricted them to those for which their international connections, their adaptability, and their acumen gave them perhaps special qualification."

▼ English Crusaders were especially cruel in their persecution of the Jews, whom they denounced for enjoying their ill-gotten wealth while the soldiers were fighting to expel Muslims from the Holy Land, and avenge the Crucifixion. Christian soldiers exterminated entire Jewish communities.

▼ All of Christian Western Europe was closed to Jews. In 1290, they were expelled from England, in 1492, from Spain, and shortly thereafter from Portugal.

▼ Martin Luther, leader of the Reformation, voiced bitter hatred for Judaism and Jews. He said Jews should be expelled from the country, forbidden to worship God, their prayerbooks and the Talmud confiscated, their synagogues burned, and their homes destroyed.

With the Reformation, however, many Christians turned from a hatred of Judaism and Jews to another kind of discrimination called philo-Semitism, which holds that Jews are the "beloved" partner not because they are Jews and practice Judaism but because they have a role in the salvation of Christians.

Philo-Semitism also finds expression in Christian Zionism, a topic explored by the Palestinian Christian Jonathan Kuttab in Chapter Nine. (p 61, 62)

Generally, fundamentalists today remain anti-Semitic—many from a "love" of Israel that makes Jews different and destined for extinction.

However, not all Christian fundamentalists have been, or now are, anti-Semitic. As might be expected of any group, there are personal and political differences among them that make generalizations inaccurate and dangerous.

Nevertheless, many fundamentalists, well-connected and respected in their own circles, have an established history of having taught their followers that Jews were behind all of the world's troubles. In the 1930s, fundamentalists including Arnold C. Gaebelein, popular Bible teacher and editor of *Our Hope,* James M. Gray, president of Moody Bible Institute, and Gerald B. Winrod, founder of the Defenders of the Christian Faith, taught that Jews were instigators of an international conspiracy.

They based their anti-Semitic statements on *The Protocols of the Learned Elders of Zion,* a series of alleged secret proceedings in which Jews plotted to destroy Christianity, undermine democratic governments, control the international economy and take over the world. Originating in Russia, the *Protocols* were first published in the United States in Henry Ford's *Dearborn Independent* in 1920 as "The International Jew." The book became a crucial part of organized anti-Semitism.

By the late 1930s, however, "Increasing numbers of fundamentalists realized that people who promoted the Protocols and the idea of an international Jewish conspiracy sounded too much like Nazi sympathizers," church historian Timothy Weber points out. "By the 1940s and the coming of the war with the indisputable evidence of Hitler's genocidal campaign against the Jews, those fundamentalists engaged in anti-Semitism backed off."

In 1948, after the founding of Israel, those who had accused Jews of an international conspiracy changed. They

Hate by Degrees

An anti-Semite "is someone who hates Jews more than he's supposed to."

—TV Evangelist James Robison

were still anti-Semitic, but in a different way. They became subtle, benign, patronizing. They became "lovingly" grateful. Jews, at last, were doing what they were supposed to do: leave Poland, Russia, Germany, England, the United States—go to Palestine, re-create an Israel.

As this melded with their dispensationalist beliefs, they became fiercely supportive of the Jewish state. They, or anyone else, might criticize France, England, Germany, Italy, the United States—*any* other country of the world. That was a matter of politics. But to criticize Israel was to criticize God.

At the same time dispensationalists speak of a love for Israel, they often reveal they have no liking for Jews.

One of the earliest of the dispensationalists, the British philanthropist, Lord Shaftesbury (1801-1885), seems typical. Known as the "Great Reformer" for his championing of more humane treatment of child labor, the mentally ill and prisoners, Shaftesbury saw Jews playing a key role in the "divine plan" of the Second Coming of Christ. As he interpreted Scripture, the Second Coming could transpire only with the Jews living in a restored Israel.

"He stressed that the Jews were vital to a Christian's hope of salvation," religion professor and ordained Presbyterian minister Donald E. Wagner points out. "Moreover, he saw commercial benefits in Jews moving to Palestine. With an English-controlled Jewish stronghold in Palestine, Shaftesbury said, Britain might outpace France in the control of the Near East; it would insure England a direct land passage to India; and, Britain would have vast commercial markets opened to its economic interests."

It was not a mere coincidence, Wagner writes in his book, *Anxious for Armageddon,* that these political goals matched those of the British Foreign Office.

"Shaftesbury was your typical dispensationalist," Wagner concludes. "He wanted all Jews to go to Palestine, create an Israel. But he didn't like Jews as Jews, calling them 'a stiff-necked, dark-hearted people, and sunk in moral degradation, obduracy and ignorance of the Gospel.'"

Armageddon—for the Jews

Standing, overlooking the Megiddo valley, Clyde, a traveling companion, explained to me that this was the site where Christ would lead the forces of good against evil. "Two-thirds of all the Jews will be killed," Clyde said, citing Zechariah 13:8-9. Pausing for some math, he comes up with nine million dead Jews. "For two hundred miles, the blood will reach to the horses' bridles."

When I express concern over this scenario, Clyde explains, "God is doing it mainly for his ancient people, the Jews. He's devised a seven-year Tribulation period mainly to purge the Jews, to get them to see the light and recognize Christ as their savior."

But why, I ask, would God have chosen a people— "God's favorite" as Clyde says—only to exterminate most of them?

"As I said, God must purge them," Clyde says. "He wants them to bow down before His only son, our Lord Jesus Christ."

But, a few will be left? To bury their dead?

"Yes," Clyde tells me. "There'll be 144,000 who are spared. Then they will convert to Christ."

Only 144,000 Jews will remain alive after the battle of Armageddon. These remaining Jews—every man, woman and child among them—will bow down to Jesus. As converted Christians, all the adults will at once begin preaching the gospel of Christ. Imagine! They will be like 144,000 Jewish Billy Grahams turned loose at once!"

—Writer-lecturer Hal Lindsey

As long as they don't convert, Jews are "spiritually blind."

—Jerry Falwell, *Listen, America*

81

Armageddon—for the Jews

I know a lot of you here today don't like Jews. And I know why. He (a Jew) can make more money accidentally than you can on purpose.

—Jerry Falwell

Who will the Antichrist be?. . . Of course he'll be Jewish.

—Jerry Falwell

"If I don't accept Christ, I'll go to hell?" a Jewish interviewer asked a Moral Majority spokesman, Dan Fore. "Yes," said Fore, that was right.

God hears the prayers of a Christian, said Bailey Smith, a former head of the Southern Baptist Convention. But, said Smith, "God does not hear the prayer of a Jew."

The world has always hated the Jew, and my heart bleeds for these people . . .

—TV Evangelist Jack Van Impe

Prophetically, the only thing that could prevent it (a Jewish holocaust) is Israel's repentance.

—Dispensationalist Dwight Pentecost in an interview with writer Paul Boyer

The statement by Rev. Jerry Falwell, that the Antichrist, who is evil incarnate, is Jewish, borders on anti-Semitism at best and is anti-Semitic at worst . . . It appears clear that after years of Christian-Jewish dialogue, Rev. Falwell hasn't learned a thing.

—National Director Abraham H. Foxman, Anti-Defamation League

12
THE CHRISTIAN RIGHT–AND AMERICAN JEWS

Traditionally, American Jews who have known discrimination were allied with others who also suffered from racism. They were liberal, supportive of liberal agendas. But in 1967 after Israel seized Arab lands, which it did not want to relinquish, the Jewish state moved increasingly to the conservative right. American Jews, seeing their number one priority as support of Israel, also moved rapidly in that direction.

"The paradox that must be recognized," Irving Howe and Bernard Rosenberg noted in *The New Conservatives*, "is that insofar as Israel functions—must function—as a state dealing with other states, its impact upon American Jews is—perhaps must be—conservative." In becoming more conservative, the American Jews recognized that the Israeli Right and the Christian Right were nationalistic and militaristic, each with a doctrine centered around Israel and a cult of land.

Nathan Perlmutter of the Anti-Defamation League of B'nai B'rith provides us with the most clearcut explanation of why U.S. Jews support the Christian Right. First, he says, he feels himself a somewhat typical American Jew in that he weighs every issue in life by one measure: "Is it good for the Jews? This question satisfied, I proceed to the secondary issues."

In the case of Jerry Falwell, liberal Jews should support him because he supports Israel. That, for Perlmutter, is the primary issue. Liberal Jews may not agree with Falwell's domestic policies on more nuclear weapons, abortion or prayer in schools. But, contends Perlmutter, these are secondary issues. In his book, *The Real Anti-Semitism in America,* Perlmutter writes:

"Jews can live with all the domestic priorities of the Christian Right on which liberal Jews differ so radically because none of these concerns is as important as Israel." Perlmutter recognizes that evangelical-fundamentalists interpret Scripture as saying all Jews eventually must accept Jesus Christ or be killed in the battle of Armageddon. But, meanwhile, he says, "We need all the friends we have to support Israel . . . If the Messiah comes, on that day we'll consider our options. Meanwhile, let's praise the Lord and pass the ammunition."

Irving Kristol, a leading spokesman for New York's Jewish intellectual community, also urges American Jews to support Jerry Falwell and other right-wing fundamentalists. He urges American Jews to forget liberalism and "join the ultra-right." Everyone is headed in that direction, he believes, adding that in this "real world" Jews are better off to back the ultra-conservatives.

Jerry Falwell, Kristol says, is "strongly pro-Israel." To be sure, he adds, occasionally a fundamentalist preacher will say that God does not hear the prayer of a Jew. But "after all, why should Jews care about the theology of a fundamentalist preacher when they do not for a moment believe that he speaks with any authority on the question of God's attentiveness to human prayer? And what do such theological abstractions matter as against the mundane fact that the same preacher is vigorously pro-Israel?"

In a world "rife with conflict and savagery," Kristol urges American Jews to be more embracing of the Religious Right's social issues.

As for politics being more important than spiritual

values, Alexander M. Schindler, a Reform rabbi and president of the Union of American Hebrew Congregations, says, "Most Jewish leaders are willing to forgive anything as long as they hear a good word about Israel."

Jacques Torczyner, an executive of the American sector of the World Zionist Organization, went further, stating it was natural for Zionists to embrace the Christian Right. "We have,

Militants Joining Militants

Douglas Krieger, an evangelical lay leader of Denver, Colorado, closely connected with Terry Reisenhoover in raising money to eradicate a mosque and build a temple in Jerusalem, early on urged Israel to work with and totally embrace evangelical-fundamentalists in exchange for their support of Israel.

In a lengthy analysis paper prepared for Israeli and American Jewish leaders, Krieger points out that as a consequence of its wars of aggression, Israel faced two choices: to seek peace by withdrawing from "territory acquired by war," to use the language of the U.N. Charter and Resolutions 242 and 338. Or to continue reliance upon even greater military strength.

If the Israelis took the second choice and continued their militaristic aggrandizement—which Krieger, as a dispensationalist urged them to do—then the Israelis and American Jews would face the danger of an outbreak of anti-Semitism.

Because of Israel's military seizure of Arab lands, "a rise of anti-Semitism could possibly surge in the West." This could be prevented, however, Krieger said, through its alliance with the New Christian Right. He pointed out that Israel could use the evangelical-fundamentalists to project through their vast radio and television networks an image of Israel that Americans would like, accept and support.

Moreover, Krieger said, "The Religious Right could sell the Americans on the idea that God wanted a militant, militarized Israel. And that the more militant Israel became, the more supportive and ecstatic in its support the U.S. Right would become."

first of all, to come to the conclusion that the right-wing reactionaries are the natural allies of Zionism, not the liberals."

Alleck Resnick, president of the Zionist Organization of America, made clear he also supports the Jewish-fundamentalist alliance. "We welcome, accept and greet such Christian support for Israel," Resnick told ZOA's June 1984 Presidential Leadership Conference in Jerusalem. Another speaker, Israel's Evangelical Liaison Harry Hurwitz, who works out of the Prime Minister's office, stressed that Israel welcomes right-wing evangelical support: "Christian fundamentalists are by and large supporters of Israel, and we are not selective when it comes to mobilizing support."

Recognizing the importance of its alliance with the Christian fundamentalists, the Rabbinical Council appointed Rabbi Abner Weiss as its liaison to the New Christian Right.

American Jewish leaders supporting an alliance with the Religious Right include Rabbi Seymour Siegel of the Jewish Theological Seminary (Conservative), Rabbi Joshua Haberman of the Washington Hebrew Congregation (Reform), Rabbi Jacob Bronner, executive director of the Belz Hasidic Community, Dr. Harold Jacobs, president of the National Council of Young Israel (Orthodox), and Rabbi David Panitz of the Anti-Defamation League of B'nai B'rith.

Militant Jewish leaders and Christian dispensationalists have formed an alliance that embraces the same dogma. This dogma is not about spiritual values or living a good life so much as it is about political power and worldly possession—about one group of people physically taking sole possession of land holy to three faiths. It is a dogma centered entirely on a small political entity—Israel. Both Jewish leaders and dispensationalists make ownership of land the highest priority in their lives, creating a cult religion—and each group is doing so cynically for its own selfish objectives.

THE
CHRISTIAN
RIGHT—
AND
POLITICS

13
THE CHRISTIAN RIGHT–AND MIDDLE EAST POLITICS

In the waning days of World War II, President Roosevelt met with King Abdul Aziz Al Sa'ud of Saudi Arabia on the high seas. Jews, persecuted under Hitler and the Nazis, Roosevelt told the Saudi King, needed a homeland. What about Palestine?

"The Palestinians did not persecute the Jews," the King told him. "The Nazis did. It is wrong to punish the Palestinians for what the Nazis did. I cannot support taking the homeland of one people to give to another."

Fundamentalist Christians felt otherwise. They said that Jews going to Palestine—where few Jews had lived for the past 2,000 years—would mean "fulfillment" of biblical prophecy.

▼ In 1948, President Truman was among the first to recognize the Jewish state. The vast majority of American Jews at that time were not pressing for a Jewish state and many, including *New York Times* publisher Arthur Hays Sulzberger, opposed it. But a few powerful Zionists gained Truman's ear—and his vote. In recognizing a Jewish state, Truman pleased the vocal and dedicated Jewish Zionists as well as a vast majority of American Christians. In doing so, however, he negated the voices of tens of millions of Arabs and Muslims around the world who opposed driving Palestinians from their homeland.

▼ In 1956, with French and English support, Israel attacked Egypt: the Israelis wanted the Sinai. The French and English wanted the Suez canal. The U.S. government, led by President Eisenhower, opposed the action. Eisenhower became the first and only U.S. President to take such bold action—going against a wide-spread belief that God sanctions—and the U.S. should sanction—whatever action Israel takes.

▼ In 1967, the U.S. began a practice of allowing American Jews to vote in Israeli elections when the U.S. Supreme Court, with Justice Abe Fortas, one of the most powerful Jewish Americans, casting a swing vote that upheld the right of Beys Afroyim, an American citizen, to vote in an Israeli Knesset election as well as other Israeli political elections. Until this decision, Section 401(e) of the 1940 Nationality Act provided that a U.S. citizen "shall lose his (U.S.) nationality by . . . voting in a political election in a foreign state."

▼ In 1967, Israel attacked its Arab neighbors. Fearing that a U.S. spy ship, the USS Liberty, then in the Mediterranean, might intervene in their territorial ambitions, the Israelis torpedoed the Liberty, killing 34 American crewmen and wounding 171. In that year I was working as a White House staff writer for President Johnson. I knew nothing about the attack. Neither did the American people. Johnson knew. But, rather than criticize Israel, he colluded with those who had killed Americans.

After torpedoing the Liberty, rendering it incapable of eavesdropping on its secret plans, Israel invaded Syria, seizing the Golan Heights. "No American official, while still in government," says James Ennes, a USS Liberty lieutenant, "has ever criticized Israel for the willful attack."

▼ In the 1967 war, Israel, in addition to the Golan Heights, also seized military control of the Sinai peninsula, territory west of the Jordan River (the West Bank), the Gaza Strip and Arab East Jerusalem. Under international law, it is not legal to occupy land seized militarily. The international law, says the religious right, applies to all nations of the world—except Israel. Jerry Falwell tells Israeli leaders they need not abide by international law.

▼ In 1980, the Israeli government, to offset disapproval of its illegal annexation of Arab East Jerusalem, fostered the creation of a right-wing Christian organization called the International Christian Embassy. The Israeli government furnished a stately former West Jerusalem Arab residence, once the home of the Said family, whose owner's nephew is the well-known Palestinian-American scholar and author Edward Said of Columbia University.

The Saids are among millions of Palestinians dispossessed of their homes and living in a disaspora.

To open the newly-created Christian Embassy, the Israelis and Christian Zionists staged ceremonies attended by leading Israeli officials and 1,000 Christians, representing 23 nations. On two occasions, I visited this Israeli-supported base for Armageddon advocates.

I met the director, Johann Luckhoff of South Africa, a Christian who said, his eyes ablaze with intensity, he'd be proud if his own son could fight Arabs—and die in an Israeli uniform. Like all dispensationalists, he's made a cult worship of the Land of Israel. In doing so, Israelis have jokingly called him "more Israeli" than any of them. From Jerusalem, Christian Embassy leaders have fanned out around the world, opening other Israeli supported Christian "embassies"—with political overtones and, some have suggested, covert missions—

Israel's 'Pre-emptive Nuclear Hit'

I had an insight briefing at NATO headquarters in Brussels, and Robin Beard, our assistant director of defense, and Robert Hunter, our ambassador to NATO, both admitted to me that they worry about . . . a nuclear confrontation in the Middle East. They believe it is inevitable . . . the (Middle East) peace process is tragic. (Israel is) heading for an inevitable nuclear exchange . . . their only hope of survival is a pre-emptive nuclear hit . . .

—Evangelist Chuck Missler on Missler Web site, 15 May, 1995.

in 37 countries throughout Europe, North America, Asia and Australia, as well as across America where there are an estimated 20 such offices.

▼ In 1982, Israel sent tanks and invaded its northern neighbor, Lebanon. Ariel Sharon led the attack. Pat Robertson rode into the fray in an Israeli jeep. In the ensuing war, Israel killed and wounded 200,000 Lebanese and Palestinians, most of them civilians. In waging the war on its neighbor, Israel, said Robertson, was doing God's will.

While Robertson did not fight in the war, Jewish American citizens donned Israeli uniforms and fought alongside Israeli soldiers. "Israel is the only country in the world that enjoys such privilege—of having American citizens fight in their wars," says a Jewish writer, Israel Shahak of Jerusalem. "By special permission of the U.S. Administration, American Jews can volunteer to serve in the Israeli army." Although "a quite large" number of American Jews "rushed to volunteer in the 1982 invasion of Lebanon, the Israeli censorship banned any mention of them and thus they were 'invisible' to the U.S. media."

▼ In March, 1985, Jerry Falwell, speaking to a conservative Rabbinical Assembly in Miami, pledged to "mobilize 70 million conservative Christians for Israel." He also took credit for converting Senator Jesse Helms of North Carolina into one of Israel's staunchest allies. Helms soon thereafter became chair of the Senate Foreign Relations Committee.

▼ In August, 1985, I attended the first of the Christian Zionist Congresses, which were instigated by Israel and Christian dispensationalists. It was held in Basel, Switzerland, in the same hall where 88 years earlier Theodor Herzl, a secular Jew and Austrian journalist, in an appeal to all Jews to live exclusively among Jews, had staged the first Jewish Zionist Congress.

I was one of 589 persons from 27 countries attending the three-day conference.

We met in sessions lasting 12 hours a day. We listened to top Israelis as well as Christian leaders. Out of a total of 36 hours we were in session, I estimated that delegates spent more than 99 percent of the time on politics. The conference had nothing to do with Christ, and was all about how Israel could support the political agenda of the dispensationalists—and they, in turn, could support the political agenda of the Israelis.

▼ In 1991, the U.S. went to war against Iraq for invading its neighbor, Kuwait.

Iraq has been bombed to what some call "the stone age." It has no nuclear weapons. Israel, according to the CIA, has had nuclear weapons since 1967, and currently stockpiles more than 200.

▼ In 1996, Netanyahu, newly elected Israeli prime minister, convened the Israel Christian Advocacy Council. He invited 17 evangelical and fundamentalist leaders to visit Israel, including Don Argue, president of the National Association of Evangelicals; Brandt Gustavson, president of the National

Israel and the Arabs

The Arab world is an Antichrist world.
—Webber and Hutchings, *Is This the Last Century?*

If the U.S. ever turns its back on Israel, we will no longer exist as a nation.
—Writer-lecturer Hal Lindsey

Theologically, any Christian has to support Israel . . . If we fail to protect Israel, we will cease to be important to God.
—Jerry Falwell

Dispensational beliefs reduce "the complex and diverse societies of Africa, Asia and the Middle East to walk-on roles as allies of Gog in God's great end-time drama . . . the consensus was clear: prophetic imperatives required the elimination of Arabs not only from (Jerusalem) but from most of the Middle East . . . They stood in the way of God's promises to the Jews."
—Paul Boyer, *When Time Shall Be No More*

Religious Broadcasters; and Donald Wildmon, president of the American Family Association. These leaders, representing several million Christians, signed a pledge expressing the hope that "America never, never desert Israel."

▼ April 10, 1997: Dispensationalist Christians placed a pro-Israel advertisement in *The New York Times,* using biblical texts for their assertion that "Jerusalem has been the spiritual and political capital of only the Jewish people for 3,000 years." Those signing the ad included Pat Robertson; Ralph Reed, then director of the Christian Coalition; E. E. McAteer of the Religious Roundtable; and Falwell.

▼ January, 1998: Falwell helped arrange a meeting between Israeli Prime Minister Netanyahu and Christian supporters of Israel, including Southern Baptist Convention leaders Morris Chapman and Richard Land as well as John Hagee of San Antonio. The Christians pledged to mobilize their communities against the Clinton administration's pressure on Israel to relinquish Palestinian lands. Falwell told Netanyahu: "There are 200,000 evangelical pastors in America and we're asking them all through e-mail, faxes, letters, telephone, to go into their pulpits and use their influence in support of the state of Israel and the prime minister."

▼ April, 1998: Prime Minister Netanyahu addressed Christian supporters of the National Unity Coalition for Israel, including Kay Arthur of Precept Ministries, the *700 Club's* Terry Meeuwsen, Southern Baptist Convention President Paige Patterson, columnist Cal Thomas, as well as Senators Trent Lott and Sam Brownback and Representatives Dick Armey, Dick Gephardt and Tom DeLay. Jerry Falwell spoke, telling Christians they must support Israel in its claim to all of Jerusalem.

▼ April, 1998: Israel and the Religious Right again joined hands. Netanyahu addressed the Voices United for Israel Conference. He pledged support to some 3,000 evangelicals, including Ralph Reed of the Christian Coalition, Kay Arthur of Precept Ministries, Jane Hanson of Women's Aglow and Brandt Gustavson of the National Religious Broadcasters. "We have no greater friends and allies than the people sitting in this room," the Israeli leader said.

▼ 1998: John Hagee, dispensationalist pastor in San Antonio, raised $1 million for Israel, to help resettle Soviet Jews in Palestinian lands. Asked if he realized that his plan went against international law, Hagee said, "I am a Bible scholar and a theologian and from my perspective, the law of

Aid to Israel

We U.S. taxpayers give the small state of Israel more than $6 billion in foreign and military aid a year. This is in addition to hundreds of millions of taxpayer dollars going to Israel from other parts of the federal budget.

U.S. aid to Israel has always been a touchy subject. Members of Congress never mention the total. Perhaps if they did, constituents would ask why Israel receives so much more federal money than do U.S. states in the same population range, and whose residents pay taxes to the federal government.

Over the past 46 years—from 1949 to 1995—U.S. taxpayers have given $62.5 billion in foreign aid to Israel. This means we've given one of the world's smallest countries—with a population less than that of Hong Kong—as much aid money as we've given all of the countries of sub-Saharan Africa and Latin America and the Caribbean combined.

The total aid to those countries amounted to $40 per person while the aid to Israel amounted to $10,775 per person.

That aid is official foreign aid. Then, outside that budget, there is a large amount of *additional* U.S. taxpayer assistance that flows to Israel. This additional money does not appear either on the U.S. AID or U.S. Foreign Assistance charts. Grants to Israel are tucked into the budgets of many U.S. agencies ranging from the Department of Commerce to the U.S. Information Agency, with the largest chunks appearing in the Pentagon budget.

If you add these additional grants, we taxpayers have given more than $83 billion to Israel, which comes out to more than $14,000 annually per present day Israeli.

—Richard Curtiss, retired career foreign service officer, editor, *Washington Report on Middle East Affairs*

God transcends the law of the United States government and the U.S. State Department."

▼ 1998: Israel canceled its obligations to live up to the Wye Peace accords with the Palestinians. Christian Coalition leaders praised Israel for being tough, for rejecting peace.

▼ 1998: President Clinton reviewed possibility of clemency for American-born Jonathan Jay Pollard who, according to U.S. authorities, stole more secrets from the U.S. than any other spy in American history. Pollard, a Jew, said he acted "in the interests of my state," meaning Israel.

▼ Feb. 25, 1999: Israel's Supreme Court ruled that an American Jew who never lived in Israel—but who fled there for sanctuary—would not be returned to the U.S. for trial. Although Israel signed an extradition agreement with the U.S., under a 1978 Israeli law, citizens of Israel cannot be extradited to stand trial abroad. The Supreme Court ruling, upholding the 1978 law, came after a Maryland resident, Samuel Sheinbein, charged with killing, dismembering and burning an acquaintance, Alfredo Enrique Tello Jr., fled to Israel. Sheinbein, U.S. prosecutor Douglas Gansler pointed out, "was born, raised, went to school and lived here his entire life."

Zionists in creating a Jewish state held to the idea that all Jews—in all countries of the world—are automatically— and first of all—citizens of that Jewish state. The 1978 ruling not to extradite Jewish citizens, according to the February 25, 1999 *New York Times,* "reflected the view that Jews should not be handed over to gentile courts." It did not matter, the Israeli Supreme Court ruled, that Sheinbein had never lived in Israel—he was a Jew, and "no further affinity with Israel is required for the appellant to be considered an Israeli citizen."

Politics of Loving Israel

No Israeli prime minister since Menachem Begin would think of making a trip to the United States without checking in with leaders of the New Christian Right in both public and private meetings . . .

The real story in the last 20 years is the founding of scores of small, grassroots, pro-Israel organizations that rarely get into the headlines. They exist to mobilize their local evangelical community to support Israel . . .

The Restoration Foundation of Atlanta puts on seminars, colloquia, and retreats to promote "the restoration of all believers to their rightful heritage in the Judaism of the first century church" and love for Israel and its people.

The Arkansas Institute of Holy Land Studies in Sherwood, Arkansas, advertises itself as a "specialty college" and offers unaccredited bachelor's and master's degrees in "Middle East History". . . Hebraic Heritage Ministries of Houston wants Christians to worship on Saturdays and observe the Jewish festivals . . .

In 1995 Ted Beckett of Colorado Springs organized the Christian Friends for Israeli Communities to provide "solidarity, comfort and aid" to Jewish settlements in the West Bank and Gaza by linking them with evangelical congregations in the United States. By 1998, there were 35 congregations involved, all of them expected to promote awareness of Israel in their communities.

—Timothy P. Weber, dean at Northern Baptist Theological Seminary and author, *Living in the Shadow of the Second Coming*

14
THE CHRISTIAN RIGHT–AND DOMESTIC POLITICS

One might think that a Middle East war—the 1967 war, when Israel won military victories over its Arab neighbors—would have little to do with U.S. domestic politics.

Yet it was that war that led Israel—and many American Jews—to exchange vows of support with U.S. dispensationalists such as Jerry Falwell and those who would eventually seize control of the largest American Protestant group, the Southern Baptist Convention.

Israel turned to the marriage of convenience with dispensationalists after it began to lose support of some liberal American Jews, who were pressuring the Jewish state to relinquish militarily-occupied Arab lands in exchange for peace agreements with its neighbors, including the Palestinians. Israel, not wanting to vacate the lands, sought support in America's corridors of power from religio-politicians such as Jerry Falwell and other dispensationalists.

"There was a shift in the politics of American support for Israel, with Christian fundamentalists picking up some of the slack left by a divided and uncertain American Jewish community," reports Allan C. Brownfeld of the American Council for Judaism.

"Until 1967, Falwell in his sermons never mentioned Israel," said Dr. James Price of Lynchburg, Va., who with Dr.

William Goodwin wrote *Jerry Falwell: An Unauthorized Profile*. Both are ordained Presbyterian ministers and college professors.

"After 1967, Falwell made Israel his main topic," Dr. Price told me in an interview I had with him and Dr. Goodwin. "The Israelis invited Falwell on an all-expense paid trip and feted him. Generals took him by helicopter over the Golan Heights. Falwell planted some trees in what became the Jerry Falwell forest and he was photographed over there, on bended knee.

"Israeli Prime Minister Begin asked Falwell to go into Palestinian lands and proclaim that God gave the West Bank to the Jews," Dr. Price continued. "So Falwell, accompanied by his bodyguards and reporters, went there and, surrounded by Jewish settlers, declared that God was kind to America only because 'America has been kind to the Jew.'

"Begin then honored Falwell at a 1980 gala dinner in New York, presenting him with Israel's highest award. No gentile had ever before been so honored. The award is named for Vladimir Ze'ev Jabotinsky, a right-wing Zionist ideologue. In 1923 he founded Betar, a militant youth organization that urged Jews to emigrate to Palestine. And he started the Jewish Haganah militia, out of which eventually evolved the Israeli army."

"Most Americans may not have heard of Jabotinsky," Dr. Goodwin now picked up the narrative. "But he provides a key to understanding why militant right-wing Israeli leaders admire Christian fundamentalists such as Falwell.

"Jabotinsky said power should be your goal. Falwell thinks like Jabotinsky." And, Dr. Goodwin concluded, "The Israelis understand that."

For my interviews with Professors Price and Goodwin, I had flown from Washington, D.C., to Falwell's home base of Lynchburg, Va. Meeting me at the airport, Dr. Price began:

"Jerry Falwell and the Christian Right have no better friend than Israel. As you came in for a landing, did you see Falwell's plane the Israelis gave him?" Although I hadn't seen

100

the plane, when in Jerusalem I had heard Falwell tell then Defense Minister Moshe Arens, "I want to thank you for that jet plane you gave me."

"There it is," said Dr. Price, pointing to a nearby hanger, with a jet out front. "It's a Windstream. It's valued anywhere from two and a half to three and a half million dollars. The spare parts came to about a half million. Our source is a pilot, who knows Falwell's pilot. Falwell boasts he travels as much as 10,000 miles in a week in this jet—recruiting voters for his favored political candidates."

As early as 1967, Falwell, perhaps encouraged by his best friends, right-wing Israeli leaders, dreamed of becoming head of America's largest Protestant organization, the Southern Baptist Convention.

It was in that same year that another dispensationalist minister, Paige Patterson of Dallas, met Paul Pressler, a Texas state appeals court judge of Houston and an ideologue with political ambitions.

In their takeover of the SBC, Patterson and Pressler, reports William Stephens, formerly of the Southern Baptist Sunday School Board, now retired, undoubtedly knew they would have the support of American Jews as well as Israeli leaders. "Thus, one driving force behind the SBC takeover was to use the Convention as a power base to affect U.S. policy toward Israel," Stephens said.

Trading Theology

The Evangelical New Right . . . systematically seized control of the leadership of the Southern Baptist Convention, the largest Protestant denomination . . . altering long-held theological positions for political advantage.

—Sidney Blumenthal, in October 22, 1984 issue of *The New Republic*

The Religious Right's increasing clout in domestic politics can be noted in these developments:

▼ Late 1970s. Jerry Falwell formed the Moral Majority, with a following dedicated to voting on domestic issues as directed. Subsequently, other, similar groups appeared, such as the Religious Roundtable, founded by E.E. McAteer of Memphis, Tenn.

Grounds for their growth were made fertile by the presidencies of Ronald Reagan and George Bush, each of whom was indebted to the New Christian Right for his election.

"The power of the Christian Right became especially clear during the Reagan Administration," says University of Virginia professor Jeffrey Hadden. "The building of the Christian Coalition began with, and is sustained by, dispensationalist radio and television preachers and their millions of followers."

President Reagan represented a dispensationalist view that since "Christ is at the door," spending on domestic issues should not be taken too seriously.

"Most of Reagan's policy decisions," said James Mills, a former California state official, were based on his "literal interpretation of biblical prophecies." This led to Reagan's idea that there was "no reason to get wrought up about the national debt if God is soon going to foreclose on the whole world."

Reagan's support of "gung-ho, neo-conservatives" can be understood, Mills said, only in the light of the president's dispensationalism. "Why be concerned about conservation? Why waste time and money preserving things for future generations . . . It follows that all domestic programs, especially those that entail capital outlay, can and should be curtailed to free up money" to wage an Armageddon war.

▼ 1980s. Throughout this decade, many Religious Right leaders moved to set political agendas on issues such as school prayers, anti-abortion, anti-euthanasia and moving the nation from a democracy to a theocracy.

▼ 1996. At the Republican convention, noted *Atlantic Monthly* writer Christopher Caldwell, "the Christian conservatives moved to make their intraparty advantage permanent and institutional." And, added the Christian Coalition's Ralph Reed, "People of faith now play a major role in policy debates and political elections."

▼ 1998. The Religious Right mustered a *majority* House vote in favor of the "Religious Freedom Amendment" to the Constitution. (This was not enough for approval, since the Constitution requires a two-thirds vote in each house and approval of three-fourths of the States.) "This so-called 'freedom' amendment," says C. Welton Gaddy of the Interfaith Alliance, is "clearly designed to subvert the separation of church and state."

▼ 1998: The Religious-Right-endorsed candidates won Senate contests in Illinois and Kentucky and hotly-contested House races in Idaho, Indiana, Ohio and Washington.

However, their candidates for governor in Alabama, Georgia, New Hampshire and South Carolina were defeated, as were their U.S. Senate candidates in North Carolina, South Carolina, Washington and Wisconsin. Because of these defeats, powerful religious broadcaster Ed Dobson calls for resignation of "the coach," and as fast as e-mail, House Speaker Newt Gingrich is gone.

The Religious Right now has "litmus tests" for judging "people of faith," Albert R. Hunt reported in a 1998 *Wall Street Journal* article. They qualify voters as "people of faith" if they vote *for* Congressional term limits, *for* a constitutional

James Watt

I do not know how many future generations we can count on before the Lord returns.

—James Watt, U.S. secretary of the interior (1982-1983) speaking before the House Interior Committee, in an apparent refutation to arguments for conserving natural resources.

amendment making it harder to raise taxes, and *for* medical savings accounts. And if they vote *against* restrictions on carrying concealed weapons, *against* the Legal Services Corporation and *against* more money for student loans.

In Texas, Hunt wrote, the Religious Right judges candidates for political office on such "Christian" issues "as a state sales tax on motor vehicles." In California, the Christian Coalition's voting guides "are even more egregious. In the last election in California, for example, candidates were deemed less committed to faith if they voted against term limits or a Constitutional amendment making it harder to raise taxes or medical savings accounts."

▼ 1999. Conservative Christians led the charge in the impeachment trial of President Clinton. Writing three months prior to the House impeachment vote, analyst Elizabeth Drew noted, "The ever-stronger Republican base, the Christian Right, demands that it happen, and few Republicans will risk crossing them." The support of the Christian Right, she said, "is more important to most Republicans than the President's job approval ratings."

Kenneth Starr, a Born Again fundamentalist from Texas, led a four-year, $50-million-dollar investigation. Starr, who attends a McLean, Virginia dispensationalist church, said he sought "truth"—and to uphold the Constitution.

"This was not about the sacred Constitution of the United States," Philip Stevens of *The Financial Times* wrote. "It wasn't even honest politics. The impeachment of Bill Clinton was personal. It was an act of vengeance."

Once Starr handed in his report, House Majority Leader Tom DeLay, a Born Again Christian from near Houston, became the chief legislative strategist behind the drive to impeach the President.

With all that was happening, he told a *New York Times* reporter, his faith sustained him. He pointed to a plaque, prominently displayed on his office wall, and referring to the End of the World: "This could be the day."

▼ 1999. Former Vice President Daniel Quayle announced he'd like to become the Republican nominee for U.S. President. Should he ever rise to such a position, he'd have a hand near "the button" and his theology as regards Armageddon becomes the business of us all.

Reporters Elinor Brecher of the Louisville, Kentucky *Courier Journal* (September 25, 1988) and Liz Smith of the New York *Daily News* (October 3, 1988) have raised questions regarding the religious convictions of both Dan and Marilyn Quayle. They reported that the parents of both are avid followers of Col. Robert B. Thieme, Jr., pastor of Berachah Church in Houston, a dispensationalist described as "far to the right of Jerry Falwell."

Reporter Suzanne Nicole in a September-October, 1990 issue of *Freedom Writer* states both Marilyn and Dan Quayle are "avid followers" of Thieme, who teaches all world peace efforts must fail since God demands a world conflagration that destroys the earth. Nicole says Thieme on occasions preaches in an Army Air Corps uniform, and that for collection plates he utilizes upside-down, camouflaged combat helmets. For church ushers, he likes uniformed Marine, Army, Air Force and Navy men.

The terrible period of Tribulation, Thieme teaches, is "the time of Satan's desperation." This will usher in the End of Time—the final battle that destroys Planet Earth. However, as a dispensationalist, Thieme tells his followers not to worry: they can be Raptured and escape the destruction.

One of Texas' most successful businessmen and a Baptist lay leader, John F. Baugh of Houston, has spoken and written extensively on how two men turned one of the nation's

The Jewish Advantage

It cannot have escaped the attention of leaders of the Religious Right that a positive relationship with the Jewish community is politically and socially advantageous.

—A. James Reichley, *Piety and Politics*

foremost religious organizations into a political base to elect candidates of their choice—and gain personal power.

Baugh, now in his 80s, is an outstanding corporate leader who, beginning only with the help of his wife, Eula Mae, personally built a successful business that became the nucleus of the nation's foremost wholesale food distributors. After corresponding with him for a couple of years, and reading his well-documented book, *The Battle for Baptist Integrity,* I flew to Houston in 1999 to personally hear his views on how politically-minded zealots seized control of the Southern Baptist Convention, the largest of all Protestant organizations.

"The hostile takeover was not about Scripture, but rather about power—and politics," Baugh told me.

"The Southern Baptist Convention had existed for some 150 years as an identifiably cohesive people of faith. During this long period, Southern Baptists upheld their major distinctive theological pillars, including: the priesthood of all believers—or soul freedom, autonomy of the local church, and separation of church and state."

Since its 1845 founding in Augusta, Georgia, "the SBC, always maintaining a sense of common theological tradition, had survived numerous debates on Scripture," Baugh said.

"Then in 1967, two men, Paul Pressler and Paige Patterson, met for the first time to plan a takeover of the SBC. In 1978, they invited other fundamentalists to join them. And the following year, at the SBC national meeting in Houston, Patterson, then president of the ultra-dispensationalist Criswell College in Dallas, and Pressler, an ideologue with vaulting ambitions not realized as a Texas state appeals court judge, seized control. They installed their candidate, dispensationalist Adrian Rogers of Memphis, as president."

And how, I asked, was the voting done?

"It's done by delegates, called 'messengers.' Until 1979, delegate votes reflected the wishes of the majority—the 90 percent *mainline* Baptists. Voting delegates never gave fundamentalists, representing the other 10 percent, any sizable vote.

"Yet, in the election of Rogers, this was turned upside

down. The SBC Executive Committee immediately reported 'irregularities.' As one example, Pressler, who had not been elected a messenger by his own church—Houston's First Baptist—nevertheless was seen casting a ballot. Confronted by this discrepancy, he claimed he was an 'honorary member' of another church, which had elected him, a violation of the SBC Constitution."

Other irregularities, Baugh said, documented by Dr. Grady Cothen in his book, *What Happened to the Southern Baptist Convention,* included some churches sending more that the legal limit of ten messengers, as well as some messengers registering twice.

"One pastor registered for himself, his wife and four children. Under questioning, he admitted that the children were not at the convention. Another pastor told of watching a man mark eleven ballots in the presidential election and turn them all in. By such tactics, the ideologues seized control of what they had not funded, supported or built," Baugh told me. Their trophies included:

▼ More than ten billion dollars in SBC assets. They

Support of Gun Lobby

Millions of fundamentalist Christians believe that the final confrontation between the forces of God and Satan will begin in their lifetimes; and, although most of them hope they will be plucked up to heaven before the battle starts, they are still unhappy at the prospect of Christians being disarmed by a government which may well be under the control of the enemy. This line of thinking explains the fundamentalists' strong support for the militia movement, which in their eyes served the dual purpose of reconnecting Americans with their historic roots while also preparing them for the apocalyptic battle to come. It also explains why millions of Bible-believing Christians identified so strongly with the Davidians (of Waco, Texas) . . .

—Damian Thompson, *The End of Time: Faith and Fear in the Shadow of the Millennium*

now control, at national SBC Nashville headquarters, the tithes, offerings—and accrued interest—of contributions donated by millions of *mainline* Baptists.

▼ Nineteen convention agencies and institutions, including the Foreign Mission Board, the Annuity Board—which holds assets in the billions of dollars in retirement funds for 50,000 to 100,000 Baptist ministers—and the Sunday School Board, the world's largest publisher of religious material and owner of Broadman Holman Press of Nashville.

▼ Six Southern Baptist Seminaries with enrollments totaling some 10,000 students. From inception, these had been funded and supported by moderate Baptists, with little, if any, support from the fundamentalists who now control them.

Having gained control of 19 convention agencies and institutions, as well as six seminaries and billions of dollars in assets, the ideologues, Baugh said, were poised to play hardball in local, state and national elections. He said they took these steps to turn the SBC into a political base:

▼ In 1982, the SBC adopted a resolution favoring an amendment to the Constitution of the United States that would empower state legislatures and local school boards to write and require the recitation of prayers in public schools.

▼ In 1986, Patterson made it clear that any potential SBC employee must state clearly he or she was anti-abortion, anti-euthanasia and pro-school prayer.

▼ In 1992, the SBC, seeking total control of the Washington, D.C., Baptist lobbying group known as the Baptist Joint Committee on Public Affairs, withheld all funds going to this group. At the same time, the SBC invested its Christian Life Commission with greater political power. It thereby negated the long-standing Southern Baptists' position calling for separation of church and state. Instead, the SBC—through its Christian Life Commission—sought tax monies for Baptist institutions, even churches.

▼ In 1988, one top SBC official, James T. Draper, campaigned actively on behalf of Pat Robertson in his bid for the Republican presidential nomination.

▼ In 1989-90, Pressler served as president of the Council for National Policy, a highly secretive, ultraconservative political think tank.

▼ In 1998, all top SBC officials eagerly sought meetings with Israeli Prime Minister Netanyahu, pledging their support for his agenda and receiving his support for theirs.

While using the SBC as a political base, the Patterson-Pressler team sought total "mind control" of all SBC employees. "We have hundreds of examples of how they forced Christians to pass their test of what it means to be a Christian," Baugh said. "They were not interested in the worker's faith, but in control of his or her mind—in gaining total loyalty to them and their political agenda.

"As an example, Wilburn T. Stancil, a popular professor at Midwestern Theological Seminary in Kansas City, held similar views on the Bible to those of the trustees. Yet, they demanded that he sign a document saying he was an 'inerrantist.' He refused. For upholding the traditional Baptist convention of 'soul freedom,' he was fired."

In the case of Russell H. Dilday, Baugh said he was elected in 1978 as president of Southwestern Seminary in Fort Worth, the largest seminary in the world. "Dilday was widely known for his brilliance and effectiveness. Yet he fearlessly called Baptists to put Christ—not politics—at the top of their agenda. On March 8,1994, the fundamentalists fired Dilday."

In seeking total mind control, the ideologues, Baugh said, "want all women subservient. In 1998, they approved a new amendment, now an article of denominational faith, stating that 'a wife is to submit graciously to the servant leadership of her husband.' All employees, men and women, wishing to retain their jobs are expected to 'reaffirm' the newly amended confession—and to do so in writing."

The Future

I do not believe it is possible for Baptists who put Christ first in their lives to stay in the fundamentalist-dispensationalist camp, where politics takes first priority.

I stand with Herbert Reynolds, Baylor University chancellor, when he challenges *mainstream* Baptists to move forward beyond the gutter politics of the Southern Baptist Convention.

Given its size, energy and economic clout—Texas Baptists gave offerings close to $100 million in 1998—the Baptist General Convention of Texas has the potential to unite many of the diverse subgroups, formally or informally, into a new Baptist entity. We Texas Baptists, representing the ninth largest denomination in America—with almost three million members—can create our own opportunities, our own paths of service.

We have not lost. In putting Christ above power and politics, we know—in the words of Baptist Toby Druin—"We have a Jesus worth following."

—John F. Baugh, Baptist lay leader of Houston
and author of *The Battle for Baptist Integrity*

The Strength of the Christian Right

The Christian Coalition in 1999 is using its $17 million annual budget to recruit 100,000 activists who will serve as Coalition liaisons to specific religious congregations . . . Within the Republican Party, the Religious Right has tremendous institutional power . . . They plan literally to hand-pick the next President of the United States.

—The Rev. C. Welton Gaddy, Executive Director,
The Interfaith Alliance, Washington, D.C.

The Religious Right represents more than a third of the Republican Party's total membership. They control the GOP organization in nearly 20 states, and are a strong force in at least a dozen others.

—William Martin, Rice University professor of sociology

Term Limits for All

America had for eight years a president (Reagan) who believed that he was living in the end time and rather hoped it might arrive during his administration.

—Frank Kermode, *Apocalypse Theory
and the End of the World*

111

EPILOGUE

The Character of Our God

Dispensationalism, a relatively new belief system—less than 200 years old—has become tremendously popular in recent years. There are four main aspects to dispensationalism.

First: those who preach Armageddon theology are anti-Semitic. Jerry Falwell and other dispensationalists profess a fervent love for Israel. No one, not even Israelis, proclaim more loudly and often their unconditional support for the Jewish state. Their support of Israel, however, does not arise out of guilt for past persecutions or even from sympathy for Jews who suffered through the Holocaust. Rather their support is based on wanting Israel "in place" as a landing base for the Second Coming of Christ. Meanwhile, Falwell and other dispensationalists speak disparagingly of Jews—as Jews.

Secondly, the dispensationalists have a narrow view of God and the six billion people on planet earth. They worship a tribal God concerned with only two peoples, Jews and Christians. They say everything that is important to them—as Christians—centers on Israel. They hold to an idea that

God has put Jews, now numbering about 14 million, on an "earthly" track. And a billion Christians are on a "heavenly" track. The other five billion peoples of the world are not really on God's radar screen until He calls them forth to be slain at Armageddon.

Despite or because of their narrow focus on God and the universe, the dispensationalists have a third characteristic: they embrace a certitude, based on an assumption that they understand the mind of God. They provide a scenario, like a movie script, that unfolds with time sequences, epochs or "dispensations"—all ending happily with an end-time escapism called the Rapture—for a chosen few like themselves.

"They appeal to those who want to feel they are on the 'inside' of a group, with secrets, profound knowledge and revelation," explains a retired Presbyterian minister, L. Humphrey Walz.

A desire for certitude, writes G.A. Wells in *Neo-Fundamentalism,* "illustrates the willingness of millions to trust in the authority of individual leaders. The authority of the great fundamentalist evangelists is far greater than that of bishops or other leaders in the institutional church, or of scholars or theologians in liberal Christianity. Their present day success in winning followers on a huge scale naturally increases their own confidence, often to the point where they suppose themselves to be really inspired."

Fatalism represents a fourth aspect. The world, say the dispensationalists, is getting steadily worse. We can do nothing. They sharply criticize the status quo, but make no effort to change it for the better. The pastors preach about a God of wrath, of vengeance and war. They declare God does not want us to work for peace, but rather *demands* that we wage a nuclear war that destroys planet earth.

A frightening by-product of teaching and believing that God has foreordained Armageddon, says British churchman Robert Jewett, "is that it is so easy to CREATE the very situation which is being described, so that the interpretation . . . brings about its own fulfillment."

"The real issue," says Stephen O'Leary, author of *Arguing the Apocalypse*, "is the way this interpretation of end-time prophecy conditions all our expectations . . . (making nuclear war seem) a perverse fulfillment of divine destiny."

In the sermons I have heard preached by Jerry Falwell, Tim LaHaye, John Hagee and other dispensationalist pastors, I have not heard any mention of Christ's universal love—or of the Sermon on the Mount.

"Jesus was no sissy!" I heard Jerry Falwell shout. He and other Armageddon theologians portray Christ as a five-star general, astride a horse, leading all the armies of the world—and, armed with nuclear warheads, slaying billions of unbelievers.

John Crossan in *The Birth of Christianity* argues that the original teachings of Jesus were nonaggressive and non-violent. Moreover, Jesus, Crossan says, taught the true faith of social equality. In a chapter entitled "The Character of Your God," Crossan says Jesus would reject any view requiring "a God of wrath and vengeance."

To create "a new heaven and a new earth," with neighbors living in peace, we can find in any great and true religion words that teach us how to treat others as we ourselves like to be treated—that is, justly, fairly, with understanding and compassion. Each of us can, then, choose to define the character of our Creator, electing to follow a God of war or a God of universal love—and peace.

Glossary

Antichrist—a personified opponent of Christians, either the devil or his human representative, who will take over the government of the world, and rule, at least for a while, with complete impunity, and whose reign will be a sign of the end of the world.

Apocalypse—From the Greek, meaning an unveiling of that which is hidden.

Apocalyptic—referring to the final world cataclysm that will destroy the powers of evil and usher in the kingdom of God.

Bible—a collection of writings, held to be of divine and human origin. Includes 39 books of the Old Testament and 27 works in the New Testament (this number varies slightly within different religious traditions). The Bible evolved over 1100 years (approximately 930 B.C. to 100 A.D.), although earlier oral and written traditions existed.

Biblical Inerrancy—belief that books found in both the Old and New Testament were dictated by God and rendered by the human scribe without error in the original autographs.

Book of Revelation—(also known as the Apocalypse) is the last book in the New Testament. Written in mystical, allegorical, highly imaginative language, it describes the events of Jesus' Second Coming at the end of time. It is the source of most "traditional" apocalyptic beliefs.

Charismatic—from the word charisma, which traditionally implied the possession of spiritual gifts. Christianity's charismatic movement encourages its followers to display expressions of emotionalism. Its leaders practice glossolalia, or speaking in tongues, unintelligible speech-like sounds viewed by some as a manifestation of deep religious experience. The fast-growing Pentecostal church is charismatic, and most charismatics also are dispensationalists. Pat Robertson is one example.

Christianity—the religion founded on the teachings of Jesus Christ and his early disciples. For most of its history, the Church and its followers believed that Christ fulfilled, superseded and replaced the old Hebraic traditions, and that the Christian Church embodies the millennial kingdom of God. This belief was universal until the advent of Christian Zionism.

Christian Zionism—belief that Jews must live in a re-created Israel before Christ can return to Jerusalem. A precursor of dispensationalism, it makes Israel the centerpiece of the world and the stage-setting for the unfolding of the End Times.

Christian Identity Movement—a movement of disparate elements of the far right, the Ku Klux Klan, neo-nazis, skinheads and the "Aryan" resistance movement, which insists that "Aryans" are the descendants of the ten Lost Tribes of Israel.

Conversion—within Protestantism, the belief that one must be "Born Again"—accept Jesus Christ as one's personal savior—in order to gain eternal bliss.

Dispensation—a time period or epoch, whereby people are judged according to their personal relationship with God.

Dispensationalism—a belief system that holds, among other things, that the signs of the Second Coming of Christ are clearly spelled out in Scripture and can be identified with current international events. This theology, less than 200 years old, was popularized by John Darby of England and in America by Cyrus Scofield, whose Scofield Reference Bible explains that God has special interest in only two peoples: Jews, said to be on an "earthly" track, and Christians on a "heavenly" track.

Dispensationalist—one who adheres to the belief in seven epochs (dispensations) that must transpire to usher in the Second Coming of Christ.

Evangelist—a title generally given Matthew, Mark, Luke and John, disciples of Christ. The Greek root word for evangelical means "one who shares the good news," i.e., the Gospel of Jesus Christ. Well-known modern-day evangelists included John Wesley and George Whitefield of Methodism, George Fox, founder of the Society of Friends, and Dwight Moody, the best-known 19th-century American evangelist. The electronic age, with the phenomena of radio, TV and the Internet, has given rise to evangelists such as Jerry Falwell and Pat Robertson, who reach audiences in the millions.

Fundamentalists—Protestants whose roots date back to 1885-1920 when doctrinal battles raged over evolution, scientific analysis and modernism. Their name derives from a series of pamphlets entitled "The Fundamentalists" (1910-1915). Such spokesmen as William Jennings Bryan defended the "fundamentals" of Christianity. A Niagara Bible Conference in 1895 listed five unalterable requirements of belief for a fundamentalist: 1) the inerrancy of the Bible; 2) the virgin birth of Jesus Christ; 3) the "atonement" given sinful mankind through Jesus' death; 4) the resurrection of Jesus after His death and burial; and 5) the "incarnation" of God, appearing on earth in human form as Jesus.

Gog and Magog—references found in the book of Ezekiel as enemies of Israel, and which dispensationalists generally have taken to mean Russia and China.

Millennium—one thousand years of godly rule on earth. Millennial preoccupation throughout history has emerged most strongly in periods of great changes that bring about social and economic upheavals. Evangelicals have held varying views as to whether the thousand years of godly rule on earth will transpire before or after the Second Coming of Christ.

Postmillennialists—those who believe mankind can and will create a righteous, godly kingdom on earth before Christ's triumphant reign on earth. The revivals of the 1730s and 1740s promoted a sense that God was then working on earth to establish His kingdom. There was a sense of self-confidence, self-determinism, and an air of optimism about the perfectibility of humanity and society. With some important exceptions, postmillennialism generally prevailed among American evangelicals until the latter half of the 19th century.

Premillennialists—those who believe Christ personally will return before the beginning of the Millennium. They believe He will be the impetus for the final battle between good and evil, establishing His millennial kingdom. They expect an imminent, apocalyptic end to human history. Premillennialists have no hopes for this world. They believe we must destroy the earth—by our own hands.

Preterist—one who believes the prophecies of the Apocalypse already have been fulfilled.

Rapture—a belief that Born Again Christians will be lifted up into heaven. Traditionally, Christians believed that, like the hero of *Pilgrim's Progress,* they must endure suffering and hardships to reach heaven's pearly gates. However, dispensationalists are taught that they need not suffer for one moment, that they will experience an instant Rapture—thus escaping all various holocausts that precede the destruction of Planet Earth.

Religious Right—represents the most visible and fastest growing branch within the evangelical movement. The term generally is used in a political connotation. After making "religious" appeals, ministers have used donations for a "political" affiliate, such as the Christian Coalition, to elect ultra-conservative political candidates.

Tribulation—generally understood to be a seven-year period of great upheaval never before experienced on earth. Dispensationalists insist that God will punish the Jews in particular during this period because of their disbelief in Christ.

Bibliography

Ateek, Naim Stifan. *Justice, and Only Justice: A Palestinian Theology of Liberation.* Maryknoll, N.Y.: Orbis Books, 1989.

Bakker, Jim. *Prosperity and the Coming Apocalypse.* Nashville: Thomas Nelson Publishers. 1998.

Baugh, John. *The Battle for Baptist Integrity.* Austin: Battle for Baptist Integrity, Publisher. 1996.

Beegle, Dewey. *Prophecy and Prediction.* Ann Arbor, Mich.: Pryor Pettengill, Publisher, 1978.

Betts, Robert B. *Christians in the Arab East.* Atlanta, Ga.: John Knox Press, 1982.

Blackstone, William E. *Jesus is Coming.* Chicago: Fleming H. Revell Co., 1908.

Boyer, Paul. *When Time Shall Be No More: Prophecy Belief in Modern American Culture.* Cambridge, Mass: Harvard University Press, 1992.

Bull, Malcolm. *Apocalypse Theory and the Ends of the World.* Oxford: Blackwell Publishers, 1995.

Canfield, Joseph M. *The Incredible Scofield and His Book.* Vallecito, CA: Ross House Books, 1998.

Cothen, Grady C. *What Happened to the Southern Baptist Convention?: A Memoir of the Controversy.* Macon, GA: Smith and Helwys, 1993.

Cragg, Kenneth. *The Arab Christian.* Louisville: Westminister-John Knox Press, 1991.

Crossan, John D. *The Birth of Christianity: Discovering What Happened in the Years Immediately After the Execution of Jesus.* San Francisco: Harper, 1999.

Falwell, Jerry. *The Fundamentalist Phenomenon.* New York: Doubleday, 1981.

Falwell, Jerry. *Listen, America.* New York: Doubleday, 1980.

Fosdick, Harry Emerson. *A Pilgrimage to Palestine.* New York: Macmillan, 1927.

Gerstner, John M. *Wrongly Dividing the Word of Truth: A Critique of Dispensationalism.* Brentwood, TN: Wolgemuth & Hyatt, 1991.

Goldmann, Nahum. *The Jewish Paradox.* New York: Grosset & Dunlap, 1978.

Bibliography

Goodman, William R., and Price, James J.H. *Jerry Falwell: An Unauthorized Profile.* Lynchburg, Va.: Paris & Associates, 1981.

Hagee, John. *Final Dawn Over Jerusalem: The World's Future Hangs in the Balance with the Battle for the Holy City.* Nashville: Thomas Nelson Publishers, 1998.

Isaacs, Stephen D. *Jews and American Politics.* Garden City, New York: Doubleday, 1974.

LaHaye, Tim and Jenkins, Jerry B. A series dealing with the Rapture: *Left Behind* (1995), *Tribulation Force* (1996), *Nicolae* (1997), and *Soul Harvest* (1998). Wheaton, Ill: Tyndale House.

Lindsey, Hal. *The Late Great Planet Earth.* Grand Rapids: Zondervan Press, 1971.

Lindsey, Hal. *The 1980s: Countdown to Armageddon.* New York: Bantam Books, 1980.

MacPherson, Dave. *The Rapture Plot.* Simpsonville, S.C.: Millennium III Publishers, 1995.

Malachy, Yona. *American Fundamentalism and Israel.* Jerusalem: The Hebrew University Press, 1978.

Marsden, George M. *Fundamentalism and American Culture: The Shaping of Twentieth-Century Evangelism, 1870-1925.* New York: Oxford University Press, 1980.

Martin, William. *With God on Our Side: The Rise of the Religious Right in America.* New York: Broadway Books, 1996.

McGinn, Bernard. *Antichrist: Two Thousand Years of the Human Fascination with Evil.* New York: Harper, 1996.

Mendel, Arthur P. *Vision and Violence.* Ann Arbor: University of Michigan Press, 1992.

Moen, Matthew C. *The Christian Right and Congress.* Tuscaloosa: The University of Alabama Press, 1989.

Nijim, Basheer K., editor. *American Church Politics and the Middle East.* Belmont, Mass.: Association of Arab-American University Graduates, 1982.

O'Leary, Stephen D. *Arguing the Apocalypse : A Theory of Millennial Rhetoric.* New York: Oxford University Press, 1998.

Perlmutter, Nathan and Ruth. *The Real Anti-Semitism in America.* New York: Arbor House, 1982.

Said, Edward. *Orientalism.* New York: Pantheon, 1978.

Scheer, Robert. *With Enough Shovels : Reagan, Bush, and Nuclear War.* New York: Random House, 1982.

Shahak, Israel. *Jewish History, Jewish Religion: The Weight of Three Thousand Years.* London: Pluto Press, 1994.

Simon, Merrill. *Jerry Falwell and the Jews.* Middle Village, N.Y.: Jonathan David Publishers, Inc., 1984.

Strozier, Charles. *Apocalypse: On the Psychology of Fundamentalism in America.* Boston: Beacon Press, 1993.

Thompson, Damian. *The End of Time: Faith and Fear in the Shadow of the Millennium.* Hanover, NH: University Press of New England, 1997.

Wagner, Donald E. *Anxious for Armageddon: A Call to Partnership for Middle Eastern and Western Christians.* Scottsdale, Penn.: Herald Press, 1984.

Weber, Timothy P. *Living in the Shadow of the Second Coming: American Premillennialism 1875-1982.* Grand Rapids, MI: Zondervan, 1983.

Wilson, Dwight. *Armageddon Now!* Tyler, Tex.: Institute for Christian Economics, 1991.

Articles:

Balmer, Randall, "'Thy Kingdom Come': Apocalyptism in American Culture." *Union Seminary Quarterly Review.* (Vol. 49, No. 1-2.)

Crowley, Dale, "Errors and Deceptions of Dispensational Teachings." *Capitol Hill Voice.* (12-part series, 1996-1997.)

Martin, William, "The Religious Right and Foreign Policy." *Foreign Policy.* (Spring, 1999.)

Minges, Patrick, "Apocalypse Now! The Realized Eschatology of the 'Christian Identity' Movement." *Union Seminary Quarterly Review.* (Vol. 49, No. 1-2.)

Wagner, Donald, "Evangelicals and Israel: Theological Roots of a Political Alliance." *The Christian Century.* (November 4, 1998.)

Weber, Timothy P., "How Evangelicals Became Israel's Best Friend." *Christianity Today.* (October 5, 1998.)

Index

For additional copies of
FORCING GOD'S HAND:
Why Millions Pray for a Quick Rapture
—And Destruction of Planet Earth

Please Contact:
CROSSROADS INTERNATIONAL PUBLISHING
P. O. Box 42058 Washington, D. C., 20015

For information on Grace Halsell's books, see her Web site:
http://members.aol.com/CRoadsInt
For E-mail: CRoadsInt@aol.com

ABOUT THE AUTHOR

Grace Halsell grew up in West Texas, studied at two Texas universities, Columbia in New York and the Sorbonne. On her first assignment overseas, she toured Europe by bicycle. Later, while writing for twelve Southwestern newspapers, she traveled in Europe, South America, Asia and the Middle East. Her dispatches have been datelined Russia, China, Korea, Vietnam, Bosnia and Kosovo

In addition to writing for U.S. newspapers, she was columnist for the *Japan Times, The Hong Kong Tiger-Standard, The Arab News,* and *La Prensa* in Lima, Peru.

She worked in the White House as staff writer for President Johnson for three years.

Her books include *Soul Sister,* which relates her experiences after darkening her skin and living as a black woman in Mississippi and Harlem; *Bessie Yellowhair,* the story of her life on a Navajo reservation in Arizona; *The Illegals,* based on her experiences among Mexicans who cross the U.S.-Mexico border without papers; and *In Their Shoes,* a memoir.

Grace Halsell is listed in *Who's Who in America.* She was named the Green Honors Chair Professor of Journalism at Texas Christian University and has received the Lifetime Achievement Award from the University of Pennsylvania.

Halsell provides a thorough examination of the strange alliance between TV evangelists and Israel's far right. Both want an end to the peace process. Both want what they term a biblically-mandated Armageddon. This book is a wake-up call for those who seek justice—and peace—in the Middle East, and for those who wish to fulfill the highest ideals of their religious faiths, whether Christian, Muslim or Jew.

—Allan C. Brownfeld, Executive Director,
The American Council for Judaism

Grace Halsell's superb work is must reading for anyone interested in better understanding the disquieting theological mindset and international goals of the Religious Right.

—Dr. Herbert Reynolds, Chancellor, Baylor University

Most Christians worship a God of peace. As Halsell's book stresses, there is a growing movement of those who—dangerously—advocate war and destruction preceded by their own safe Rapture.

—Dr. Ronald B. Flowers, Professor of Religion,
Texas Christian University

In Forcing God's Hand—activating their quick Rapture and Armageddon—Christian zealots are demanding immediate destruction of Jerusalem's most holy Islamic shrine. Halsell exposes this most preposterous "Christian" doctrine—that a Third Temple must be built in Jerusalem, that animal sacrifices be resumed, and that Jesus Christ preside on a Jewish throne—to carry out Old Testament rituals.

—Andrew T. Killgore, publisher,
Washington Report on Middle East Affair

Halsell shows that a better way to usher in "a new heaven and a new earth" is to focus on revolutionary philosophies taught by Jesus, such as loving one's neighbor.

—Jim Jones, Fort Worth Star-Telegram